The Disposable Visionary

The Disposable Visionary

A Survival Guide for Change Agents

Bill Jerome and Curtis Powell

Illustrated by Carin Powell

 PRAEGER™

An Imprint of ABC-CLIO, LLC

Santa Barbara, California • Denver, Colorado

Library of Congress Cataloging-in-Publication Data

Powell, Curtis (Marketing researcher)
    The disposable visionary : a survival guide for change agents / Curtis Powell, Bill Jerome.
       pages cm
    Includes bibliographical references.
    ISBN 978-1-4408-4036-4 (hardback) — ISBN 978-1-4408-4037-1 (e-book)   1. Organizational change.   2. Industrial management.   3. Leadership.   I. Jerome, Bill.   II. Title.
    HD58.8.P69 2016
    658.4'06—dc23   2015030216

ISBN: 978-1-4408-4036-4
EISBN: 978-1-4408-4037-1

20 19 18 17 16   1 2 3 4 5

This book is also available on the World Wide Web as an eBook.
Visit www.abc-clio.com for details.

Praeger
An Imprint of ABC-CLIO, LLC

ABC-CLIO, LLC
130 Cremona Drive, P.O. Box 1911
Santa Barbara, California 93116-1911

This book is printed on acid-free paper ∞

Manufactured in the United States of America

Copyright Acknowledgments

Illustrations courtesy of Carin Powell.
Captions written by Bill Jerome.

Contents

Preface:
What Are Companies Afraid Of?

At the beginning of their careers, the authors had the privilege of working for a start-up division of one of the country's most progressive and successful financial organizations in the world. It comprised an amazing collection of idea-generating, risk-taking, breakthrough-thinking, uninhibited individuals that, in three short years, created a $4 billion national powerhouse. And in those days, billions were worth something.

Interestingly, none of the management or the staff had any financial or banking background. It was a collection of managers whose experience included package goods, soft drinks, advertising agencies, retail, sales, and research. Yet despite their lack of conventional industry experience—or perhaps because of it—they succeeded. Their unique vision was unhindered by the organization's cultural history, internal obstacles, or political game playing. It was a great environment for two young managers who didn't fully appreciate their supervisor's observation, "Remember this time. There may not be another opportunity for you to be in an environment with such passion, brainpower, and potential to see your ideas become reality. We will change this industry. Enjoy it while you can."

Sure enough, the industry was changed. The term "home equity" was created, a national banking presence was established, breakthroughs in financial marketing were introduced, and the industry was never the same.

Since that time, the authors have worked with many other organizations and an incredible diversity of smart and innovative people. More often than not, however, their supervisor's words rang true: they seldom found an environment that welcomed, encouraged, and supported change and innovation as the standard for success. Sure, there were the minor projects or initiatives that showed some promise, but usually nothing that really moved the needle or created true breakthroughs.

Over the years, they witnessed again and again what happened to change agents and innovators who tried to push for something dramatic. Too often these visionaries were seen as troublemakers, non-team players, or people who just didn't fit the mold. They were usually fired. They took their same passion to another company—maybe even a company that said they wanted change—and soon found themselves labeled again and searching for a new position once more. It was not their lack of talent. It was usually internal politics, persistence of the status quo, and a reluctance to shake traditions that resulted in their termination. At the same time, those who perfected the art of political gamesmanship seemed to survive and thrive.

This book is dedicated to those who, despite conflicts and frustration, display the courage to challenge a company's tradition and politics and management's resistance to change. When passion meets opportunity, great things happen. We look forward to helping those driven by passion to understand how they differ from others, the rules of working within a politically driven environment, and the steps necessary to work effectively with those who may be threatened by the very actions necessary to propel the company to new levels of achievement. We also hope to open the eyes of those who can provide the opportunity to empower and unleash the power of innovation of a different breed of employee—the visionary who simply wants to make a difference.

Acknowledgments

We are all the sum of our parts and our partners. In undertaking the development and publication of *The Disposable Visionary*, the authors had help from many sources, including clients, business associates, family, and friends. First and foremost, we would like to thank and dedicate this book to our wives, Jacquee Jerome and Scottie Kersta-Wilson, for their unwavering support throughout this most unconventional journey. Their patience, endurance, and support have made all of this possible and words can't express our gratitude.

Very special thanks to Carin Powell, our talented illustrator, for visually expressing the unique combination of humor and pathos experienced by visionaries every day. Many thanks to Steve Hutson, for championing this book, to Hilary Claggett and the team at ABC-CLIO for their vision and consummate professionalism, to James Autry for his sage advice early on in this project, and to Dr. Caitlin Powell, assistant professor of psychology at Saint Mary's College of California, for pointing us in the right direction. In addition, we would like to recognize the inspirational management style of Bill Hayter, who influenced both authors with his ability to manage an eclectic group of visionaries and his unselfish philosophy of "only hire people you're willing to work for." Personal thanks as well to Tommy Smothers, whose early contact affirmed the message of this book.

Bill would also like to thank his father and lifelong mentor, Robert Jerome, whose example of perseverance and creativity has been a consistent inspiration to always pursue the best you can be in any situation. He is also eternally grateful, literally, to Jesus Christ, the ultimate change agent, in Whom he became a new creation.

Curt would also like to dedicate his portion of this book to his parents, Cecil and Mary Powell, who taught him vision, values, and persistence in the face of absurdity.

Introduction: The Dream, the Research, and the Disposable Visionary

One of the authors has a recurring dream, which he describes like this:

"In my dream I am a dog who lives with a wonderful family in a snug little bungalow somewhere in the Midwest. My favorite place to nap is the screened-in back porch facing a lush, green yard chock full of trees. In the dream, I wake up suddenly from my nap because I've sensed a change in the weather. With my keen ears, sharp eyes, and excellent sense of smell, I realize something awful is about to happen. I know with absolute certainty that a tornado has just formed and that, although the sky is clear and there are no warning sirens, the tornado is coming straight for the house and will destroy it in a matter of minutes.

I immediately run through the doggy door that connects the porch to the kitchen and dash through to the dining room where my family is having breakfast. My job is to warn them of danger, of course, and I now use every means at my disposal to do so, barking a frantic warning and running, first in circles, then back and forth between the porch and the dining room so they'll follow me and see the danger. The kids start laughing at my behavior, but behind the laughter, I start to see a glimmer of recognition on their faces that something's not quite right, so I redouble my efforts—barking, circling, running back and forth, and even growling to communicate the seriousness of the situation.

Both parents look at each other in bewilderment. The mother says, 'What's gotten into you? Is there a rabbit in the backyard? You're spoiling our breakfast!' The father starts to get up from the table, and I'm overjoyed. He knows! He understands me! He picks me up, says, 'We can't have you spoiling our meal,' carries me out through the kitchen, tosses me out onto the back porch, then shuts and locks the doggy door."

Aside from annoying one's spouse with whimpering and twitching, this dream can also serve another purpose. It's a great metaphor for the dilemma of the disposable visionary.

The concepts, examples, and ideas in this book didn't spring fully formed from a dream, though. There are many layers of research that form the backbone of the authors' approach to this subject, and if you are a visionary, it's important that you have a working knowledge of what that means to your career and your future prospects. We also like to present things in a humorous manner, because in the words of the late visionary Robin Williams, "In the process of looking for comedy, you have to be deeply honest. And in doing that, you'll find out here's the other side. You'll be looking under the rock occasionally for the laughter."[1]

IN OTHER WORDS, THERE'S A LOT OF PAIN OUT THERE

The trade press is full of articles that bemoan the lack of engagement among employees in the United States and around the world. In 2013, Gallup published research showing that in the United States and Canada, only 29 percent of employees are actively engaged in a company's activity and progress, 54 percent are not engaged, and 18 percent are actively disengaged.[2] For those readers familiar with the Net Promoter Score (NPS)[3] methodology for loyalty research, that translates to a positive NPS of only 11 out of 100, or 29 percent engaged employees minus 18 percent actively disengaged employees. Engaged employees promote their companies to other prospective employees, while actively disengaged employees spread the bad word. The "not engaged" or passives are not factored into the score for the United States and Canada. By the same logic, the worldwide NPS score is *negative* 11, with only 13 percent engaged and 24 percent actively disengaged. So much for the effectiveness of outsourcing.

Next time you're in a tug-of-war contest, try winning when a third of your team is pulling, half aren't touching the rope, and a fifth are tugging hard in the opposite direction. If you need confirmation of how this may be impacting your present company, just check out the anonymous reviews on popular job sites, where you'll encounter colorful company descriptors such as "the slow boiling frog" from employees who currently work there.

A May 2013 *Harvard Business Review* article by Rob Goffey and Gareth Jones titled "Creating the Best Workplace on Earth"[4] tells us why we should care—a lot. "Companies with highly engaged people outperform firms with the most disengaged folks by 54 percent in employee retention, by 89 percent in customer satisfaction and by *fourfold* [italics added] in revenue growth."

"Wow, Sheila! That's quite a company you've built. How many people work there?"

"Oh, about a third of them."

Why?

The article goes on to say, "Recent research . . . shows that employees who feel welcome to express their authentic selves at work exhibit higher levels of organizational commitment, individual performance, and propensity to help others."

Here's the irony of this research: if you were intrigued by the title of this book, chances are good that you have visionary tendencies. And visionaries, as explained in Chapters 1 to 6, are often, hands down, the most engaged, conscientious employees in any organization. They're also often the first to be shown the door.

Will it get any better? Not likely, according to Charles Seaford of the New Economics Foundation.[5] Job insecurity, driven by the use of temporary workers to boost productivity, is increasing in all of the developed countries regardless of improvements in their economies. The revolving door is turning faster.

BUT WHY DO VISIONARIES, IN PARTICULAR, STRUGGLE?

There's a growing body of biological, psychological, and neurological research that provides some strong indications as to why visionaries have a greater degree of lack of appreciation and job instability. We go into depth on that topic in Chapter 3, but here's a preview.

FIGHT VERSUS FLIGHT

Neurological research shows that our species is hardwired to make split-second decisions about whether any given situation is a threat or an opportunity. Like our hunter-gatherer forebears, we react to potential threats as something either to be feared (flight) or challenged (fight). For those who live in constant fear of losing their jobs, the challenge isn't worth it. Their resources and adrenaline are devoted to maintaining the status quo; that is, employment. Visionaries, though, tend to perceive scary situations as opportunities for a type of self-disruption; that is, changing things before a competitor or external force does it for you. They seem to lack the flight response that tells most employees to preserve their own jobs at all costs. Instead, they rush headlong into challenges or fight mode while the other employees around them are rushing for cover.

Neurological research show that this is the result of something called the "amygdala hijack," which is referenced in Daniel Goleman's *Emotional Intelligence*.[6] The amygdala regulates fight-or-flight response, and when the adrenaline starts flowing, the more rational prefrontal cortex takes a backseat to the unfolding drama. That's when you see the visionary's boss leaving the meeting, shaking her head and muttering, "Did I just hear him say that the only solution is a complete overhaul of our pricing model?"

THE POWER OF POLITICS

In Chapter 3 we'll cite a peer-reviewed psychological research study published by Blickle et al. in the 2012 *Journal of Organizational Behavior*[7] that examines the factors that predict job success. It's no surprise that people who have high levels of learning ability, openness to new experiences, conscientiousness, and political skill have good job performance. Surprisingly, the researchers also discovered that people with marginal ability in each of these areas had acceptable job performance ratings as well. Who struggles the most? It was the people with high conscientiousness, high learning ability, and low political skills; that is, the people with passion, vision, and no emergency brake whatsoever. Do you know anyone like that?

THE "CON" IN CONSENSUS

The Corporate Executive Board (CEB) has done extensive research into the increasing dysfunction of decision-making in organizations.[8] Unlike a decade or more ago, when managers had more budgetary, hiring, and purchasing autonomy, today's organizations require an average of 5.4 managers reaching consensus to make a decision. The 5.4 typically hail from different functional areas within the company and often have conflicting goals, motivations, and perspectives. In that type of environment, the result is not bad decision-making, it's no decision-making whatsoever—keeping the status quo. The second alternative chosen by the 5.4 is to proceed with the least risky, lowest-cost path forward. Quality and customer impact take a backseat to price. Business-to-business marketers and salespersons in any industry testify firsthand how this trend creates enormous obstacles to change and innovation.

AUTHOR RESEARCH AND FIELD EXPERIENCE

In addition to the Gallup engagement surveys, psychological studies, and corporate performance research cited, the authors also surveyed managers who were hired specifically for the role of change agent.[9] All but one revealed that they wanted to leave a job at some point in their careers. Half them were senior-level executives, and 25 percent were former or current CEOs. Our findings reinforced and expanded on the neurological, psychological, and organizational research. Although 80 percent had at some point left a job involuntarily, it turns out that only 18 percent were let go because they didn't meet performance expectations. Overwhelmingly, the reason most were shown the door was some form of political dysfunction, as measured by inability to get along with the boss, losing in power plays, standing up for other employees instead of themselves, and focusing on results instead of gamesmanship.

BUT WAIT, THERE'S MORE

The authors go into greater detail on all this research, but the conclusions are also backed up by both authors' direct experiences as managers, senior executives, and consultants for more than 100 different organizations. The vignettes presented throughout this book are pulled from real people and real situations, whose names and companies have been changed to protect the companies and their management, as well as the authors. The solutions offered have been tried and tested by both authors and within an extensive network of managers in a broad range of industries, including financial services, healthcare, education, durable goods, consumer goods, entertainment, pharmaceuticals, automotive, executive coaching, research, analytics, and high tech, just to name a few.

A VISIONARY SPURNED IS A FORCE TO BE RECKONED WITH

Ninety-eight percent of the respondents in the author research said they wanted to leave their jobs at one time or another, 51 percent because the political environment was too stifling and 48 percent because management would say one thing and do another. Only 30 percent wanted to leave because of compensation. All of the respondents were very successful but had achieved their success in short-term stints, by finding companies that value vision, or in some cases, by eventually working for themselves.

We researched historical visionaries as well, and we saw example after example of recognized leaders who were discounted at one point in their careers and went on to change companies, industries, and the world, sometimes at a cost to their former employers. These historical vignettes are meant to inform and to inspire. The traits that visionaries share—their persistence, their lack of fear in the face of failure, and their focus on doing the right thing—are all traits that make them, and you, valuable to any employer in any organization, even if you don't realize it.

YOU ARE THE PROBLEM AND THE ANSWER

Whether or not you consider yourself to be a visionary, prepare to celebrate your strengths and minimize your weaknesses. Journey through this book with a sense of self-examination and self-discovery, laughter, and tears, and you will emerge the stronger for it. And if you truly are a visionary, the world will be made stronger too.

Chapter 1

Filet o' Talent: The Gutting of Corporate America

Why we get rid of the employees we need most

When all else fails, lower your standards.

Bumper sticker

This book was written because we live in a disposable society. We use things and then throw them away. We discard things that should last longer, but we don't want to fix them. We replace things with new models, or we simply get tired of them. It's amazing what you see in the trash can or on the curb: furniture, cell phones, charcoal grills, unused exercise equipment, self-help books, even automobiles and an occasional old boyfriend.

We even watch disposable television, surfing from one channel to another, giving the show three seconds to prove its worth before we discard it for another and another and another.

Disposability is often just a matter of time frames. At one point, something is seen as very valuable: we spend time and money on it, at the expense of other things. Later, those same things are seen as useless or worse: as distracting clutter that actually gets in the way.

Some companies treat their employees the same way. They spend a lot of time interviewing prospective hires, sizing up their talent and potential, training them, asking them to sit in meetings, telling them how to do things, and getting them to conform to the company way. Later, these same companies spend weeks or months documenting why these employees, on whom they've spent so much effort, are going to be let go. Then they spend about five minutes actually getting rid of them. Just like desks, file cabinets, and computers, some employees are being dropped by the side of the road. We employee-surf just as we channel-surf: checking them out to see if they immediately give us what we are looking for, and if not, switching and moving on.

Some companies make employee-surfing routine, looking for the extraordinary employee and dropping that special hire that once was worth their time to interview and money to hire but is now seen as dispensable. They are considered the expendable ones that just didn't perform as expected.

Are these employees really the bottom of the barrel? The under-performers? Outplacement firms, headhunters, and employment agencies are often amazed at the talent that comes through the door. Many of these discarded employees have a lot to offer. Often . . . no, *usually*, these employees offer more value than those employees who were retained. So what happened? Why are these talented individuals—at one time sought, valued, and paid a premium to employ—suddenly discarded like Enron stock?

These are the questions that drive this book. Is good talent going bad, or is there something else at work? Do the employees need to change, or do managers need to adjust how they evaluate and stimulate talent?

Two clues to this dilemma have surfaced. The first clue is that some of the most talented individuals find themselves over and over again in Pursuit of Other Opportunities. This is sometimes referred to by the acronym POO, such as "The discharged employee found himself in deep POO." For the sake of propriety, the authors will try to avoid this abbreviation. The second clue is that the same companies tend to wonder why so many promising hires don't live up to their potential.

This is nothing new. It has happened throughout history. Interestingly, it has also happened to many people who later used their talent to single-handedly change a company, a country, or quite literally the world.

An examination of this recurring theme reveals an odd coincidence: a lot of talented employees were pouring out of these organizations, but new ideas, innovations, breakthrough concepts, or tremendous growth were not. Later, many of these discarded employees were able to provide great results to other organizations, on their own, or by joining with other expendable employees.

There must be a cause behind this pattern of employment, or lack thereof. It's not an individual's lack of talent, passion, or drive. It's not the company's lack of desire to have productive employees. Therefore, there must be some underlying element common to these individuals. And there might also be something common to the organizations.

Could such a common element be identified or documented?

It was on a Tuesday in May 2000 that one of the authors, having been on the phone with a number of executives who were either Pursuing Other Opportunities or frustrated with their current jobs, began to understand just how prevalent this situation had become. Upon further examination, it also became clear that people long on talent traditionally did not last long in their organizations.

And it wasn't because of lack of work or effort, but the opposite: these employees wanted to enhance their organizations, to identify and pursue new opportunities, to challenge others to expand their approach, and to work in a way that positively impacted the organization and its customers.

The core of the problem is this: Organizations say they want progress, but they don't really want to change. They try reorganizations, draft new mission statements, or issue declarations that "the customer comes first." But they don't address what really drives an organization: where the power really lies, how risk is accepted, if self-promotion is recognized or encouraged over selfless contributions, and how unwritten traditions become obstacles to change and improvement. This is why companies constantly seek out employees with talent but cannot accept their contributions or potential, so they fire them and start again.

Thought leaders in organizational behavior confirm this cycle. Companies are, on the surface, anxious for the potential impact of candidates with drive, talent, and a track record of success. But according to Warner Burke, professor of psychology at Columbia University, "Half of all executives fail or are fired, and estimates of incompetent leadership range from 30 to 67 percent. A full 70 percent of organization change efforts fail."[1] The Corporate Leadership Council reported that "nearly half of new executive hires quit or are fired within the first 18 months at a new employer."[2] Many organizations just aren't ready for the changes and challenges that change agents bring to the table.

And those who don't want change will create a culture that resists it. Politics becomes all-important, and with that shift, the inability of politics and change to coexist becomes prevalent. This is the impasse: Those employees with the greatest vision don't have the time or ability to worry about politics; those companies comfortable with the status quo can't deal with the many things that are necessary to focus, stimulate, and implement progressive change.

"And we have our winner!"

Here's some author research that illustrates the pervasive nature of internal resistance to change.[3] In speaking with employees who were once hired to institute change, enhance performance, or take on the role of change agent, many found that it was not their skills but their confrontation with politics that resulted in their dismissal or Pursuit of Other Opportunities:

- 64 percent said politics got in the way of what they were hired to do
- 51 percent said they faced a stifling political environment
- 48 percent stated that management said one thing but did another, citing an inconsistency in direction and commitment
- 34 percent faced an environment resisting new ideas

The result is that visionary employees get fired. and companies fail to progress as far as they should.

As a standard of measurement, success is no longer what employees achieve; instead it is how they fit in. As organizational politics grow, productivity decreases. Many of the most talented employees are simply unable to adapt to these new standards. Some find it uncomfortable bending that low. When they refuse to conform to the rules of survival in these politically charged environments, their subsequent dismissal can be seen as almost self-inflicted. In fact, 75 percent of those hired to enhance said, "I don't play political games, often at my own risk." And the same number agreed with the statement, "I believe in championing a good idea, even if it puts me at odds with others."

A pattern is seen in this group of otherwise intelligent, industrious, and motivated people. They often commit the political equivalent of suicide in their jobs by speaking out too much and too often. They push for change. They pursue the corporate vision, often with greater zeal than their managers. They make others in their organization uncomfortable. Most find themselves in a desperate and difficult search for a work environment that will not only tolerate them but also celebrate their value. While employed, they are unceasingly innovative, constantly questioning the status quo, challenging fundamental assumptions about the business, and helping to create or reinforce the vision of the company.

Their passion is not always welcomed, understood, or long suffered. In return for their persistence for improvement, they are rewarded with labels such as "disruptive," "uncooperative," "intolerant," and "insensitive."

These people suffer from a condition known as Disposable Visionary Syndrome, or DVS—a trait that is common among employees with a drive for change and innovation. It is usually accompanied with a headstrong belief that others will recognize the need for radical approaches and appreciate new improvements regardless of the potential conflict with current procedures, organizational cultures, or management preferences.

Perceived as employees who just don't fit in, DVS sufferers are compelled to pursue a vision for the highest level of innovation that, more often than not, exceeds that of "normal" employees and most management. If present in an environment that resists change or challenges to the status quo, the condition can degenerate into CMS, or Chronic Malcontent Syndrome, as the employee's strength of vision is suffocated by a mounting frustration over others who just "don't get it."

Misdiagnosed as "non-team players" or "troublemakers," these employees do not fit into the corporate mold and are usually shown the door, leaving the rest of the company to get moldier. No longer seen as valuable employees, the resulting conflict makes these individuals and their passion for innovation regarded as obstructive, insensitive, and easily disposable.

Considering its symptoms and eventual outcome, Disposable Visionary Syndrome might also be called "Compulsive Visionary Disorder," reflecting an obsession to always pursue a new level of what is possible. Another term might be "Status Quo Deficiency," since they are unable to be content with inefficient, insufficient, or inadequate ways to view problems and solutions. Based on the predictable outcome when management feels threatened, it could realistically be labeled "Job or Employment Deficit Disorder." This last label describes the normal outcome of most visionaries who continue to challenge the status quo and butt heads with managers who fail to see the value of new ideas. However, the same managers may have no problem seeing the challenge and disruption to a company that new ideas may

> **Disposable Visionary Syndrome (DVS)**—an intellectual/emotional/environmentally induced condition, whose symptoms begin with a compulsive desire to promote innovation and ideas to a company, with or without the support of the organization's leadership, culture, and history. It is most prevalent in employees with high vision/ high conscientiousness and low political skills. This condition is compounded when confronted with a culture that promotes the status quo. A combination of factors often leads to the termination of the employee who, thus impacted, is said to suffer from the effects of Disposable Visionary Syndrome. Throughout the book, the terms "disposable visionary" or "DVS employee" are used alternately to refer to those who exhibit symptoms.
>
> In some cases, Disposable Visionary Syndrome does not need to be terminal, either for the employee or the ability of organizations to innovate. When DVS is properly managed, the organization and the individual benefit, resulting in greater long-term growth and success.

bring. For this reason, so many visionaries have found themselves ignored or unwanted. Thus they become easily disposable.

Perhaps it's best to take a moment and look at a parable we like to call . . .

THE BOAT-ROCKER'S LAMENT, OR WHO CHEESED MY MOVE?

For the last five, ten, fifteen years, a gradual cloning evolved in corporate America. Everyone in the business started looking the same. They talked the same. They worked the same. They even came up with the same ideas. They laughed at the same jokes. They went to the same places after work. They built on each other's sameness.

And when they weren't around, they talked behind each other's backs the same. They developed their own departmental silos in the same way. They all schmoozed up to the boss the same. They all protected their butts the same.

In the corporate ship (or down in the company galley, if you prefer), they all thought they were so unique, but they all took their seats and rowed the same. The company boat glided through the water. But day after day, it went the same way. The same direction. The same speed. Often in the same circles.

And every once in a while, some new people might come along. They stood out. They didn't fit the same mold. Oh, they might have a lot in common in experience or dress. They might even be really good rowers too, and they immediately pitched in. They contributed. But something was different. Every once in a while, they stood up. They rocked the boat.

They were not content merely keeping up with the crowd. They didn't necessarily set out to be different from the crowd, but they had a different focus. They wanted to move the crowd. They had vision. They saw that the boat could move faster. They saw that there was a better way of rowing. They may have seen that rowing wasn't even necessary. Heck, wind-filled sails and outboard motors do have a purpose, after all.

But it was hard to shift a boat's direction when most of the rowers were already moving in sync with each other and were content with the status quo. They had been rowing the same way for years. Management seemed happy with the way they were going. They even received bonuses for it. And if you didn't mind being chained to your seat, there was even job security.

So when a boat-rocker stood up, he was told to sit down. If he kept standing up, he kept hearing voices telling him to sit down. And while standing, he may have pointed out other directions the boat could take. The others kept telling him to sit down. He made them feel uneasy. He was just told to row harder, but not too much harder. Finally, the row-master got fed up and tried to put him in irons. The boat rocker resisted, so he was unceremoniously thrown overboard. The other rowers were relieved and got back to rowing—the same way and in the same direction. They made steady time, even great time. Funny, though—other ships kept passing them. Some from their native land. Some from foreign countries.

A small craft carrying the commander of the fleet pulled up beside the boat. The commander stepped up and asked, "What happened to that rower we hired from that village of headhunters in our last stopover? He had so much promise!"

"Well," the row-master answered, "we just couldn't get him to fit in."

"Fit in? I thought we wanted him because he had new ideas to help us move this boat faster! Those headhunters told us he had real promise. In fact, when we talked to him, didn't we tell him we wanted him to help us move faster?"

"Yes, but he couldn't accept how we do things. He kept standing up. We couldn't keep our timing when he was rocking the boat. He kept asking questions that messed up our usual pace. He kept suggesting new directions. He questioned everything, from our rhythm to our equipment. He even asked why we don't wear gloves to prevent calluses."

"Say, why don't we wear gloves to prevent calluses?"

"We got rid of them when we went business casual. But the big problem is that he just wasn't a team player. We got tired of his interruptions. In the end, we felt we rowed better without him."

"So you just threw him overboard?"

"Yes, but we gave him a life preserver that should keep him afloat for 60 days."

"Boy, we're spending a lot on life preservers lately. That's the fifth one we've tossed this year. It sure is hard to get and keep good help these days, isn't it?"

"Sure is, sir. Every year it gets harder to retrain—oops, I mean retain talent. But you can be assured we have things back to normal now."

The commander left, and the crew resumed rowing. And nobody really noticed that most of the time, the boat was going in circles.

That new rower had shown so much promise. But instead of providing food for thought, he became food for sharks. When hired, he was seen as up-and-coming, but then he was over and out. The sharks that followed the boat didn't care. They just knew that lunch came their way on a regular basis.

On the surface, as opposed to where the sharks were, it appeared that the discarded employee had a sort of death wish. He certainly was not a team player. It looked like he had his own agenda. But in truth, he couldn't help it. He was driven by vision. Possessed by a gnawing passion to achieve the best for the company, he ultimately failed to look out for himself.

End of story.

Or does this have to be the end?

Companies don't have to succumb to the status quo or to political preferences. And change agents may want to examine some flexibility in changing themselves as well, to better fit in or to understand how to navigate waters infested with political minefields. Without some adjustment, these conflicts may continue to result in shattered careers and missed opportunities.

On a personal level, why should anyone care? The following story, drawn from a real situation, with names changed to protect privacy, provides a further clue:

BARBARA'S STORY

Even prior to working at Megabank, Barbara was viewed as a free spirit, an independent thinker, and a loose cannon. When project teams were formed, Barbara was often the last to be picked. People just weren't sure where she was coming from. Early in her career, she had been a product manager for a well-known toy manufacturer. When sales around their core product began to decline, she asked, "Why do we only focus on girls? Last time I checked, half the kids out there are boys." She then proposed and introduced a new category: a line of steroid-enhanced male action figures that completely changed the toy industry. Spin-offs into cartoons, live action movies, and numerous licensing agreements were all in the future.

Unfortunately, Barbara's job wasn't. She soon found herself Pursuing Other Opportunities.

Megabank's managers considered themselves pioneers and were anxious to employ someone who didn't fit the traditional banker mold. They eagerly hired Barbara to bring new thinking to Megabank's financial products.

But Barbara didn't fit in well. She was viewed as an eccentric. The other managers labeled her "off the wall" and "space cadet" because she didn't approach things with a traditional banker's perspective. They disliked her because she seemed oblivious to office politics and protocol. And what in the world did she know about banking? A typical meeting with Barbara was often peppered with questions that distracted from the written agenda. Eyes would roll, people would shrug, and everyone present would steel themselves for one of her crazy questions, like, "If we really want to grow, why focus most of our efforts on operational minutiae instead of sales?" Her questions made others uncomfortable. They just didn't understand her sometimes. Other times she made them nervous by driving home issues that they had ignored or just never thought about.

One day, Barbara asked a question that had bothered her from the beginning: "Everyone likes money . . . why do we make it so hard for them to get it when they need it?" And then Barbara invented the first home equity line of credit. She drove home the core issue: "Why do we make people apply for different loans when we can pre-approve them once for a line of credit? We can make it easy for them to get the money when they need it . . . and even when they don't!" The idea was such a radical departure from the old way of doing things that it took the rest of her coworkers several weeks to truly understand what she was suggesting. Just like the male action figures, this crazy idea, from an unlikely source, spawned an entire industry that's still going strong 30 years later.

But even though she had demonstrated insight and vision, Barbara still didn't fit in well with the culture of the company. Management thought they wanted new thinking, but she made them nervous. Six months after setting the company on a new path to success, Barbara was asked to leave Megabank. It was almost one year to the day after she had left the toy company for the same reason.

Barbara had a fresh perspective, dedication to the customer, and the ability to create revolutionary new concepts that made millions for her employers. But Barbara, it turns out, also had something else: she suffered from Disposable Visionary Syndrome, or DVS.

"We have a great succession plan at this company. We bring in people with great ideas, teach them to conform, fire them when they don't contribute, and promote those who've been around for years."

SO WHERE DO WE GO FROM HERE?

Disposable Visionary Syndrome does not need to be terminal, either to the employment of the employee or to the innovative possibilities of an organization. Through the following chapters, this book seeks to give hope to those with DVS, detailing its symptoms and how it relates to corporate America. It seeks to help these visionary sufferers come to a better under-standing of their uniqueness within a corporate setting, to create pride in that uniqueness, to help them identify with those who have gone on to successfully leverage this condition, and to prescribe positive steps to turn DVS from a perceived problem into a real advantage.

In addition, it will guide managers who find themselves in the challenging position of properly channeling the boundless energy, enthusiasm, and constant pressure for improvement exhibited by visionary employees. Understanding the positive motivation of the highest-potential performers and the negative messages cultural politics sends will enable leadership to be more effective in channeling and integrating this valuable energy. Chapter 10 is devoted to specific management guidelines that will maximize the impact of visionary employees and will enable them to act as catalysts for greater productivity within an entire organization.

Leveraging individual strengths of all employees, especially those with high visionary passion but low political gamesmanship, within a culture of empowerment and innovation, requires openness on both sides of the desk. If applied, there is incredible potential for growth and market-changing potential. If not, well, then you may find copies of this book lying by the curb . . . along with some of the company's most valuable employees.

So what does this mean?

If you are a visionary, you must understand and accept the fact that organizations are often in conflict with themselves. There is a desire for change and impact, but there are short-term pressures that do not always allow for the time that focused change can require. And change can bring discomfort. Recognize that change takes time and that companies really do want what the visionary employee brings, whether they immediately recognize it or not.

Chapter 2

So What Was the Problem?
What happened to that wonderful employee I hired?

Wherever you see a successful business, someone once made a courageous decision.

Peter Drucker

Visionary employees with high potential, a passion for improvement, and an apparent disregard for the corporate status quo do not have a conscious death wish. However, they do have a number of common characteristics, and there are symptoms that seem to be common in some of the potentially finest employees, innovators, and contributors in any organization.

They bring incredible drive and passion to any company they work for. But before they can fully contribute their potential to an organization, they end up getting fired or they leave, giving rise to the name of their condition: Disposable Visionary Syndrome.

Referred to in this book as DVS, this condition reflects an almost suicidal tendency from a career perspective. These employees rock the boat. They speak their mind. They are also willing to buy the Brooklyn Bridge of corporate America—that is, they usually believe what they hear from management:

- They actually believe it when a company says they want to change.
- They don't laugh when a boss says, "We don't bow down to politics here."
- They think there is truth to the statement, "You should focus on beating the competition outside, not the guy in next cube."

It's bad enough they listen to these platitudes when their colleagues apparently know better, but to make matters worse, they usually act on their beliefs. They throw out the first serve, not even realizing they are in a game. And their peers, supervisors, and executives (who assume the roles of opponents when they are supposed to be their teammates) follow with a rapid return of obstacles, defenses, and potshots. These weapons are masterfully wielded by so-called pragmatists who justify the status quo.

Their returns are often dubbed "the company line," coming in all shapes and sizes and designed to defuse the boat-rockers and the idea-challengers.

Some of these retorts are quick and to the point. Some are more obscure, which disguises their true nature, and some add to the confusion by contradicting themselves. In the face of change and progress, they comprise the corporate obstacle course designed to protect the status quo:

> The **"pass the buck" hurdle:** "Have you run this through the normal channels?"
> The **"tried and true" block:** "We don't do things like that here."
> The **"clock's running out" barrier:** "It's too late to consider other ideas now."
> The **razzle-dazzle:** "No one's ever done it that way before." Immediately followed by, "Someone must have already done that."
> The **storage locker strategy:** "Maybe we'll consider that at a later time."
> The **"not really wiser, but we'll make them think I am" bluff:** "When you've been around a little longer, you'll understand why we can't go that way."
> The **teamwork scapegoat:** "I'm not sure the other departments will be comfortable with that."
> **Or the team podiatry ploy:** "Let's make sure the other departments are on board before we consider that. We don't want to step on each other's toes."

Yet, in spite of all these obstacles, employees with vision but with low political skills still see what can be. They've never really grasped the corporate translation guide, which clearly explains that when they hear, "That's interesting, but it's not us," it really means, "The only change we like around here is in the vending machines . . . and even there, our machines only take bills."

Unflustered and with the fortitude that comes only with political innocence, DVS employees still follow ideas and strategies that they see as perfectly logical and potentially breakthrough. And soon, they rock the boat once too often, and they find themselves adrift in the sea, waiting for another boat to pick them up, where they may repeat the cycle once again.

It's not their fault. They were probably born with it. And it is fostered by a childlike belief that what is good for the customer is good for the company. Since DVS employees regard politics, bureaucracy, and committee roadblocks as irrelevant for the customer, they tend to ignore them. There is only so much you can focus on, so they skip the minutiae and look to the future.

Disposable Visionary Syndrome is a paradoxical combination of internal values. It is a mixture of Forrest Gump and Thomas Edison, a childlike faith with great vision, a political naiveté with the strength of purpose and foresight that crushes obstacles, a lack of inhibitions and an equal lack of patience with those who don't get it.

But in the end, it's usually the disposable visionary who gets it: the sack, the boot, the pink slip, the excuse for downsizing, and the severance. Disposable visionaries are the reason many HR people spend more time documenting people than they do ensuring that their managers know how to motivate them.

And so, the boat continues to row. The drumbeat of complacency and the mantra of conformity continue. The boat is stable and calm once again, sometimes moving slowly ahead, sometimes adrift, sometimes going in circles. The row-master is content. He has his routine. He just doesn't have his potentially most important rower.

So what does this mean?

One of the biggest threats to a company may be its own traditions and complacency. As a visionary, you can maintain a focus on what matters and instill that vision in others. In turn, understand that others may not see the same things you see, or they may peer through tinted glasses that have been fogged by years spent as an organizational insider.

J. C. PENNEY

RETAIL REVOLUTION: DO WHAT IS FAIR; DO WHAT IS RIGHT

Over 100 years ago, the retail industry was revolutionized due to one man's vision: to serve the public to its complete satisfaction by providing the best value at the best price. He was fired for that vision.

At the turn of the century, it was common practice not to pre-price merchandise, but instead to charge different customers different prices based on what the salesman thought each customer could afford. James Cash (J. C.) Penney saw this as profit gouging and urged that set prices be placed on the merchandise so all customers could receive a fair price. He perceived that treating customers and employees fairly would result in an explosion of business. This suggestion and his passion for it were not well received by his boss, who refused to consider the concept, and Penney was immediately fired.

However, he did find two other businessmen who shared his vision for fairness and extraordinary customer regard. Under the name "The Golden Rule Store," Penney and his investors began a new concept in both retail and service. His ideas were revolutionary: At a time when most mining communities were dependent on high-margin and disreputable credit establishments, he insisted on cash-only transactions, which allowed him to keep his costs low and prevented customers from buying beyond their means. He even insisted that the company pay cash for their inventory, allowing additional discounts, which he passed on to the customer. So deep was his concern for the customer that he resisted taking credit cards in his J. C. Penney stores until the 1960s. At that time, he grudgingly accepted his board's recommendation to use credit cards. He empowered his managers and, recognizing the value of talent, said, "I will have no man work for me who has not the capacity to become a partner."

His commitment to fairness and value was documented in a symbolic anecdote. After walking into a Milwaukee J. C. Penney store, he noticed a pair of corduroy pants marked at $3.98. He called the store manager and said, "These pants sell at $2.98!" When the manager replied, "But Mr. Penney, they are an excellent buy at this price," Penney exploded, saying, "You violated company policy! You must give the customer the best value and make a reasonable profit!" He would never deviate from his commitment not to make an excess profit at the expense of the customer.

J. C. Penney recouped his initial investment during his first year. From 1902 to 1920, his single store grew to 197 stores. By the time of his death in 1971, his company had expanded to 1,612 stores. Due to an unwavering personal example, and his credo, "Does it square with what is right and just?" his vision was caught and internalized by his employees, including one Sam Walton. Walton, who began as a Penney employee in 1940, used that same vision to create Walmart. The last time we checked, Mr. Walton's full commitment to his mentor's example was creating its own success.[1,2]

Chapter 3

Visionary Employees:
Are They Born or Made?

It's in the brain: Why some people are passionate about vision while others are preoccupied with politics

But the most pathetic person in the world is someone who has sight but no vision.

Helen Keller

In most companies, the vision provided by the DVS employee is not considered normal. That attitude is to be expected. Companies don't come in contact with it very often, and when they do, they prefer to limit, contain, or exterminate it, rather than leverage it.

But from the disposable visionary's perspective, does he or she really want to get fired, even if it means leaving a frustrating and stifling environment? Well, even a moth continues to circle a flame until it burns itself up. Similarly, DVS employees would prefer to make a difference from the inside as an employed contributor, even if it may eventually lead to their own downfall or burnout.

But why should someone pursue a path of such risk that flies in the face of normal corporate behavior? Perhaps there is something that seemingly doesn't connect in a visionary's brain. Despite their ability to see what "could be," they often overlook the obvious "what is." DVS employees often miss or ignore the connection between politics and stability. Between yes-saying and paycheck-getting. Between self-promotion and getting promoted.

Instead, they prefer to focus on the connections between revolutions and breakthrough solutions. They change their stance and swing for the fences. They rock the boat and knock down traditions. They break down silos and beat up the competition.

But this focus comes at such a price. Can people so attuned to new possibilities actually be so ignorant of politics? Can those who so clearly see what the future could hold for the company also fail to perceive what is happening so obviously around them? Well, yes, and with medical and behavioral science, it can be proposed that DVS employees actually have brains that work differently from the brains of employees who tend to prefer political survival over visionary risk. The evidence is strong that people exhibit different brain-related behaviors that explain why different people react differently in the same situations.

The reason behind these differences may not be completely clear. It could be that some people grew up in environments that encouraged or restrained breaking the mold. Perhaps it is innate personality that affects an individual's perception of danger, and so while some see playing it safe as common sense, others get a rush from living life to the fullest.

One element of the neurological basis for DVS behavior can be reflected in the flight-or-fight response. When danger is perceived, some prefer to stand and address it. Perhaps they believe they need to protect others. Perhaps they feel compelled to make things better for others in the future. They may even get a rush out of the challenge itself.

Others, however, are clearly more risk-averse. They prefer to flee in order to live and fight, or just live, another day.

In both cases, however, the analysis is the same: people see danger, and they react instinctively. The action taken is controlled by a part of the brain called the amygdala. It responds to danger. It creates an emotional response that drives instinctive behavior. It can actually block rational thinking. This is called the "amygdala hijack."[1] It explains the common phrase "so scared that he could not think straight."

How does this relate to the DVS employee? Well, imagine a meeting when a potentially visionary idea is proposed. Raised before a committee, it is at risk of being ignored or defeated due to the shortsightedness or prejudice of others. The fear of the lost opportunity or the risk of the idea failing to be even considered may create such an arousal that the DVS employee does not think straight concerning the consequences of his actions on others or on his own career. It is just like a villager who, when faced with the danger of a hungry tiger, may put the welfare of others before himself. He does not back down. He does not step back and think about the consequences. He simply, bravely (to his thinking), and perhaps foolishly (to the thinking of others) commits to the fight.

The perfect example of conflicting fight-or-flee ideology can be seen in the First Continental Congress. The revolutionaries, led by John Adams, Benjamin Franklin, Thomas Jefferson, and Richard Henry Lee, among others, saw the window of independence shrinking and were willing to put everything they had at risk. The prospect of losing this vision created a greater fear than losing anything they possessed. It wasn't a job that they were risking; it was their lives, their positions, and their future. On the other hand, the conservatives were more fearful of losing their property, the security of British protection, and their social positions. It was not that much different from the political players in today's corporate world who are more afraid of losing their job security. Adams and company threw caution to the wind. Their passion for a vision of independence overwhelmed their ability to conceive that opposition could be considered. And yet, with all their passion and debate, there were others who never agreed with their position. The resolution for independence was only accepted after Adams and his contingent were able to divide the groupthink of the more conservative representatives, persuading some, but not all, to shift their value of what was most important to pursue.

Perceptions and ingrained values of what is worth fighting for will always differ among individuals. The cause of this difference may never be known with certainty, but its existence is undeniable, and its effect will always be evident.

In today's corporate world, the DVS employee is akin to the mother bear that sees her young threatened. Instinctively, she puts herself on the line for the life of her cub, or in this case, the idea she has birthed or envisioned.

Then, on the other hand, there are other employees who view danger from a different perspective. They also react with strong resolve. But they have a different set of fears. To many employees, speaking up and disagreeing, promoting a contrary idea, or fighting the political environment creates the greatest danger. For them, they are too scared to think straight when they perceive situations that may endanger their job. It may explain why some employees seldom present or support new ideas on the spot. It may explain why arguments tend to focus on maintaining the status quo. It may explain why some people aren't willing to think outside the box. Backed into a corner by something challenging their comfort level, they also lash out—often simply to resist the threat of change to their position or to the status quo with which they have grown very accustomed. Their focus on self-preservation prevents them, at least for a short time, from thinking at all.[2]

This may also explain why management often does not appear to respond logically when faced with a potentially powerful idea that also challenges the status quo, questions current policies or requires major change. The overwhelming danger of the unknown and new approaches can stun the brain.

Psychologists explain that when people are faced with perceived danger, they will revert to what naturally drives them. They will protect what is most important to them, and they will respond with attitudes with which they are most comfortable. People with a passion for vision, progress, and ideas will seek to promote their ideas. Those driven by politics or relationships will be more likely to blend into the woodwork or simply tell people what they want to hear. The concept of being open to new thinking, for any type of person, is very difficult in such a stressful environment.

That is the rational thinking of today's psychologists. But can this be taken further? Of course it can! It provides the basis for the idea that people who are driven by ideas will not heed what others consider very common-sense warnings for job security. It reinforces the idea that DVS employees will face employment deficit challenges. It is the way their brains operate, conditioned and reinforced over time. To them, the greater risk is in doing nothing and enabling the status quo to continue.

CARLA'S AND JASON'S STORIES

Carla, a proven innovator, brought an attractive vision, independence, and a refreshing can-do attitude to the typically staid wing of a healthcare division. When the company hired a new VP of marketing, the VP hired Jason to run the day-to-day operations. Jason was known for his ability to run an organization in a safe, dependable, and non-disruptive manner. On the other hand, Carla was tapped by the new VP to join marketing because of her demonstrated ability to envision new processes and to doggedly pursue their implementation, something that was a struggle for the department Jason inherited. Carla immediately sized up the marketing challenge and in short order piloted an innovative program that would efficiently boost sales and increase customer loyalty.

The program fully integrated marketing with the service and sales departments, making sure that service concerns were addressed front and center before any attempts at sales were made. It featured a content-driven strategy that sought to solve customer problems and featured telemarketing that encouraged truthful conversations instead of canned sales pitches. And the best part? Carla had harnessed the power of predictive modeling to precisely determine which customers would be most receptive. Instead of pestering the entire customer base with email and phone calls, a much smaller percentage of customers was contacted—only those for whom the offer would be highly relevant. Because she could monitor and quickly pivot the approach based on early results. Carla's program made the traditional marketing operation look like the slow-moving, inefficient dinosaur that it was. Her program was so efficient that it was funded by the excess slush that typically sloshed around Jason's substantial budget. The VP was thrilled with Carla's early results, and he told her to expand the program, largely because Carla had proven with unshakable metrics that it worked far better and far more efficiently than Jason's status-quo programs. Jason's department, on the other hand, always seemed to require increasingly large budgets and more employees to achieve unimpressive results.

There were other differences between Carla and Jason that reflected a lot about their thought processes. Carla expressed very little fear about losing her job and, when challenged about the sustainability of her new program, told the VP without hesitation that things were going so well that the program could continue to produce stellar results with or without her; that is, it was running itself. In Carla's mind, she had presented the company with a proven, efficient process that proved her value to the company. In the VP's mind, it meant something else.

Jason, on the other hand, was so focused on self-preservation and fearful about losing his job that he literally built a human shield. How? By downplaying the abilities of the employees he inherited and by stressing the need to hire even more people to compensate for increasingly marginal results. Consequently, Jason's budget, department, and influence continued to swell, as did the company's dependence on him, while Carla's department ran on fumes and produced miracles.

What happened? When the senior execs had their annual "trimming the fat" meeting, they chose Carla in a heartbeat. Why? Because her program could run without her, while Jason's swollen bureaucracy would fall into chaos without him at the helm. Fear won the day, and Carla accepted her fate with grace and puzzlement.

But what about people like Jason, those who seem to always have the ability to weather the internal storms? Those who, as portrayed in the musical *How to Succeed in Business Without Really Trying*, always play it the company way? Those who always seem to survive the downsizing and the reorganizations? Those who feel that the greater risk is to speak up and promote possible change?

These survival-driven employees have brains that think differently from the DVS brain. They are not driven by ideas but by self-preservation. When they face the opportunity to present a new, potentially revolutionary idea or to risk challenging the status quo, they are more likely to ask, "Why Imperil My Position?" Or "Why Involve Me Politically?" This employee could also be profiled with the slogan, "Waffling Is My Policy." They also have a "Weak Instinct for More Productivity." Whichever is most appropriate, they all point to a WIMP attitude that places more emphasis on playing the right political games and avoiding risks that may rock the boat. But they survive.

These surviving employees may have brains that are more politically driven and more reactive to the environment than proactive to opportunities, so let's call them "politically astute reactionaries" (PAR employees). They see what is customary and acceptable, and they follow that path. The function of this brain enables the employee to get things done, but most often at a very standard level of performance and with little or incremental change.

Experience, goals, and a sense of value and sacrifice will determine the actions people take when they perceive danger. Those same factors that influence fight-or-flight decisions will impact the DVS and the PAR brain differently when facing corporate challenges. Driven by different perspectives, it is understandable that they might perceive opportunities and risks differently, might develop different habits and attitudes, and might even interpret the same words they hear differently. This is described in more detail in Chapter 4.

The following section presents a research-based explanation as to why the PAR and DVS brains act so differently and how those differences specifically impact job performance in an organizational or corporate setting.

THE WAY, THE WHY, AND THE WHOA

In the preface we discussed the power of politics and briefly summarized the 2012 behavioral study by Blickle et al.[3] This research examined three personality traits that accurately predict job performance as perceived by supervisors, for whom job performance usually means task accomplishment, not idea generation or revolutionary impact. And that definition of job performance raises an important point. Unless you are fortunate enough to work for a visionary supervisor, his or her perception of good job performance will generally equate to "more of the same" mediocre results, using the same methods. We discussed this in Chapters 1 and 2. Even great bosses are more likely to be evolutionaries, not revolutionaries, so if they really don't understand the value of change, their perceptions of what constitutes job performance could differ substantially from yours. Remember the "dog on the porch" dream in the preface?

As an example of what is considered nominally acceptable job performance, consider this employee performance evaluation form from a major public university, used to evaluate the support staff, that included technology, marketing, teaching innovation, and, believe it or not, excellence in performance. This evaluation was used for all employees, up to the highest director level. You will not see anything that values new ideas, initiative, or excellence. The seven key attributes that they value most are as follows:

1. The employee is positive and enthusiastic toward work responsibilities.
2. The employee gets along well and works effectively with staff.
3. The employee is patient, responsive, competent, and tactful with internal and external customers.
4. The employee completes work on time and takes special care to prevent errors.
5. The employee is flexible with responsibilities and able to shift focus easily.
6. The employee is willing and eager to assist when needed with any program.
7. The employee responds within 24 hours to email, voice mail, and phone messages.

The university culture was obviously one of mediocrity and complacency. These questions are reminiscent of an elementary school report card with the bottom-line comment, "Johnny plays well with others." And this type of evaluation is not restricted to higher education. It's not surprising that, according to Leadership IQ, only 15 percent of employees believe that their jobs lead to achieving great results.[4]

Job performance evaluations often do not address key progressive traits such as, "Does the employee always put the future of the organization first? Does the employee bring effective, innovative ideas to the company? Does the employee make other employees better? Does the employee overcome obstacles and challenge issues that prevent the maximum performance of the organization?" It is important to note the absence of traits that truly measure the employee's value to the company and, instead, the emphasis on get-long, go-along traits when supervisors are asked to review employee performance.

With that perspective in mind, we can evaluate the research and the underlying factors that others consider keys to acceptable performance. According to Blickle's research, based on personality traits, there must be other programming that stimulates the different behaviors of the DVS and PAR managers, and sure enough, that seems to be the case. The research looked at three variables that seem to predict what is acceptable performance and what is deemed as low performance. We'll call them vision, conscientiousness, and political skill.

1. **Vision:** The researchers labeled this as learning ability and openness to new experiences. In order to score high on this personality trait, the respondent would strongly agree with the following: "I read quickly; I like to read; I have a rich vocabulary; I am quick to understand things; I catch on to things quickly; I can handle a lot of information." If this seems like a job description for Google, that's no accident. Be careful, though. This view of "vision" seems to equate more to openness to new ideas than to intelligence or the actual ability to create and present new ideas. After all, there are different types of intelligence, and you can have a high IQ even if you don't like to read. Just ask any TV or film producer. Turns out, you can also have high vision and low job ratings.

2. **Conscientiousness:** The positive values of this personality trait relate to factors like competence, order, dutifulness, achievement, striving, self-discipline, and deliberation. Surprisingly, these values were not lifted from a scouting organization's handbook or a monastic order. Blickle's research was actually done in a specific European country, one known for engineering. You would think that conscientiousness is a good predictor of job ratings, but the research demonstrates that it is the mix of conscientiousness with the other traits that matters most.

3. **Political Skill:** This personality trait is the least applied by visionaries, yet in many ways it is considered the most important to traditional success. It includes obvious factors such as "I am particularly good at sensing the motivations and hidden agendas of others" and "I spend a lot of time and effort at work networking with others." But there's another, less obvious factor that the researchers call "apparent sincerity." Disposable visionaries tend to struggle mightily with this last factor, and it is often their coup de grâce. You can translate it this way: To be successful in politics, the employee must not only sense others' agendas (e.g., your supervisor's) but also excel at hiding any hint of ulterior motives in his or her own agenda. And what is that agenda? Is it driven by concern for the company, improving performance, or self-interest? Research in 2014 by the Corporate Executive Board[5] (CEB) revealed that for business purchasing decisions, the people making the decisions are almost twice as likely to be motivated by "identity value," or what it will mean for them personally, over the benefit to the company or to job performance. So when a politically

astute CIO says, "Buying this software platform will vastly increase our productivity as a company," he's really thinking, "I made the safe choice, so at least I won't get fired, and the CEO's up for retirement in two years." We'll examine this phenomenon in more detail in the next chapter.

For a passionate visionary, this type of self-serving thinking and the ability to keep from saying it out loud are foreign concepts.

What Blickle et al. found is that the relative application and strength of each of these traits have a very real impact on a supervisor's perception of an employee's performance. Vision has the least impact on most supervisors' evaluation of value. However, the interaction of conscientiousness and political skills drive perceived value by management.

Table 3.1

Employee Ranking: What the Research Shows[1] $\bigcirc$ = High $\bigcirc$ = Low				
Job Performance Ranking[2] (1–4, where 1=highest)	1	2	3	4
Learning Ability (intellectual, curious, imaginative, and open to new ideas)	⬆	⬇	⬇	⬆
Political Skill (ability to convince others of apparent sincerity)	⬆	⬇	⬆	⬇

[1]*Journal of Organizational Behavior*, 34, 1145–1164 (2013). Published online December 11, 2012, in Wiley Online Library (wileyonlinelibrary.com). doi:10.1002/job.1843. "The Interactive Effects of Conscientiousness, Openness to Experience, and Political Skill on Job Performance in Complex Jobs: The Importance of Context," G. Blickle, J. A. Meurs, A. Wihler, C. Ewen, A. Plies, and S. Gunther. In their research, the authors refer to openness to new ideas and learning ability.

[2]The job performance rankings in this chart apply only to test subjects who scored high in Conscientiousness.

Our Interpretation of the Results				
We Call These Employees	Safe Achiever	Mediocrat	Politically Astute Reactionary	Disposable Visionary
How They Operate	Understand what's important, but pick their battles carefully	Stay under the radar, do the job, and avoid politics	Be sensitive to the boss's perceptions, and avoid rocking the boat	Pursue what is right for the company with little regard for self-preservation

Here's a quick interpretation of how these results translate, from the authors' perspectives, based on our own research and experience:

> **Safe Achievers**: These professionals are naturally gifted and have high levels of all three personality traits; vision, conscientiousness, and political skill. They seem to be able to effortlessly find balance with the company's priorities and their own vision. They work hard and accomplish the supervisor's priorities. They also have an uncanny knack for reading the boss's mind, which comes in very handy at review time. But do they rock the boat? Apparently not enough to scare the boss. His or her feet may get a little wet from time to time, but the Safe Achiever is very adept at understanding and producing what the boss wants, which is more of the same, with acceptable levels of incremental change. The steady, safe performers get the highest reviews.

> **Mediocrats**: Supervisors, not surprisingly, seem to value professionals who show up day after day and get the job done, even if they have low vision and low political skills. They may or may not be particularly conscientious. In the research, that didn't seem to matter in their job performance ratings, but at least they're consistent. Boat-rocking makes these professionals feel nauseous, because it leads to less of the same and more work for them. If you looked at their performance over time, there would be no blips and no dips, just a flat line. When review time comes around, the boss gives them a solid "average" or "met expectations."

Up until now, the research hasn't told us anything we didn't already know on some level, but when we look at the PAR employees and the visionaries, things get interesting.

> **Politically Astute Reactionaries (PAR Employees)**: With low vision and high political skills, these professional-level employees are adept at "apparent sincerity," which means that they can tell it like it should be, not necessarily how it is. The boss may suspect that something's not quite right, but it's difficult for him or her to put a finger on just what it is. After all, the PAR employees seem so darn sincere. In a strange twist, the more conscientious they are and the harder they actually work, the lower their job performance is rated. That could be because the more work they produce, the more opportunities their supervisor

has to truly evaluate their "apparent sincerity." But the PAR's instinct for self-preservation, that flight factor previously discussed, is a finely tuned instrument of job preservation. That's why they are particularly toxic for and can contribute to their fellow professionals' Disposable Visionary Syndrome. It turns out that some smoke and mirrors, delivered with "apparent sincerity," makes the difference between a good review and a marginal one for the PAR employee. The diagnosis of the PAR brain tends to be appropriate in two ways. First, these employees tend to respond as reactionaries—reacting on the basis of what is politically correct rather than taking a proactive approach. Second, their performance tends to be average . . . on PAR with what is expected by the organization.

Visionaries (Potential DVS Sufferers): Possessed with an abundance of vision and low political skills, these professionals seem to rock the boat the minute they step foot in the office. At first that generates a high evaluation of job performance by their supervisor, almost approaching superstar status. But like the PAR employees, the research shows that the more conscientious the visionaries are, the less the boss thinks of them.[6] Our research shows why that might be. Unlike the PAR employees, visionaries are motivated less by self-interest and more by doing what's right for the company, but they just don't know when to stop. The more changes they make, the more their supervisor's head starts spinning and the lower their job rating goes. During the honeymoon period, it starts wonderfully, exceeding expectations, but it dips down sharply as real change starts to occur.

Add to this the visionary's strong tendency to ignore the political cues or warning signs around them, and you have the perfect breeding environment for Disposable Visionary Syndrome.

So how might brain functions be linked to or explain how different employees view opportunities and interpret political implications? The brain is often characterized as having three primary functional elements. These might be summarized as voluntary (what we direct), involuntary or conditional (what our brain does on its own, based on habit or personality), and sensory (how we react to our surroundings) activity. In light of the above research, let's take a nonscientific look at the potential differences between the way PAR and visionary brains work.

Personal Outlook:

What is good for the customer and the company . . . should be good for me.

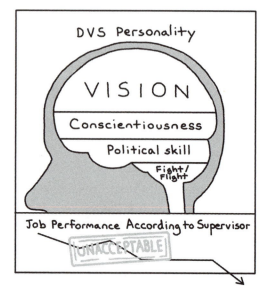

THE DISPOSABLE VISIONARY SYNDROME (DVS) BRAIN

Personal Outlook:

What is good for me . . . is good for me.

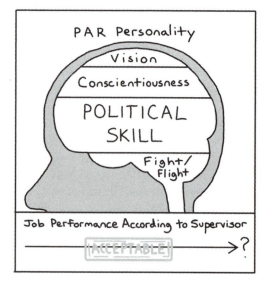

THE POLITICALLY ASTUTE REACTIVE (PAR) BRAIN

Applying a business diagnosis, the brain's three functions might be perceived as follows:

THE WAY, THE WHY, AND THE WHOA

1. Setting goals, objectives and visions: in essence, establishing the path or the **WAY** the employee wants to pursue his or her actions. This function aligns nicely with the personality trait labeled as "vision" above.
2. Responding to internal motives and behaviors that are naturally part of his or her personality: the **WHY** behind their actions. This seems to correspond with conscientiousness.
3. Reacting to the political and cultural environment and what might determine which actions to take or not take. This could be described as warning signs to **WHOA**, or reconsider. It can also give someone the freedom to confidently move ahead, having weighed the risks. As discussed, both the reaction and the outcome depend on the employee's level of political skill.

These three functional areas help describe the differences between the actions behind visionary change agents and their more conservative coworkers.

THE WAY

All employees make some conscious decision concerning their perceived role in a company. It may be a combination of what they were told their job entails plus what they personally want to achieve. It may be a position—to be CEO or just to be employed. It may be prestige (e.g., to run a large department) or it may be reward (to enjoy large salary increases). The goals just listed involve a rather narrow focus on the personal outcome of the employee. Some goals may be bigger and corporate-focused, such as creating industry-changing products or services, establishing perceptions that the company is indispensable to its customers, or implementing initiatives that preempt the competition.

Whatever the goals, they are created through a voluntary function in the brain—we make conscious decisions about where we want to go and how we want to get there. There may be influences that impact our focus, but it is up to the individual to determine his or her destination.

This is the direction and goal-setting area of the brain, and might be summarized for the layman as the WAY—the long-term journey and the measurement of success.

The research seems to indicate that PAR employees have limited or short-term vision. They see the obvious, with very focused attention on the here and now. They are attuned to filter out anything except the predictable and the nonthreatening. They see an assignment for what it is and how it can be safely accomplished. People who developed the university evaluation mentioned earlier love this attitude.

The brain of a disposable visionary, on the other hand, perceives long-term potential and a range of possibilities. While it also generally recognizes near-term opportunities, it tends to focus past them and move on to what could be possible.

We've also seen substantial differences in the fight-or-flight responses between PAR and DVS employees. For PAR employees, the focus is less on fighting major fires and more on fleeing the big ones while stamping out the smaller daily brushfires, in an "apparently sincere" manner. The DVS employee is looking at how to prevent major flare-ups down the road, so the fires serve as both challenges to fight and flames of passion that keep the vision alive.

Both views are necessary to maintain a company, but the DVS employee's vision and viewpoint can be misinterpreted as ignorant or apathetic about the smaller issues. It may be viewed as indifference to the daily needs of the company, when it's simply a longer perception of what is the most important path. It's a vision thing. Many won't understand it.

The low level of political skill of the visionary can reflect the innocence of the inner child in each of us. As we grow older, our childlike qualities adjust to preferences and beliefs.

DVS employees tend to hold on to optimistic tenets: do what is right, share, trust and believe in others, support others, and play fair. There is both innocence and vulnerability in this unselfish way of thinking. But it is a refreshing approach to life. It encourages and empowers others. It gives others credit. It takes what people say at face value. It trusts. It is the Charlie Brown in us that focuses on kicking that football over the wall when Lucy, with apparent sincerity, says, "Trust me."

When a disposable visionary's brain hears a company say, "We want to excel at all we do," it believes that statement to be true and, combined with high vision and conscientiousness, this causes the DVS employee to concentrate on excellence and to find ways to break through the ordinary. It not only perceives that direction as permission to rock the boat but also believes that there is almost a mandate to push things to the edge.

To the disposable visionary's way of thinking, if it is right to share with others, then others should naturally want to share as well. But that can often be a fundamentally bad assumption: Others may not see things the same way. They may not like to share, especially when it comes to giving credit to others. They may prefer to keep the ball for themselves. Non-DVS or PAR employees tend to focus on the "me" aspect. Their inner child's cry of "I want it. I want it now. I want to be first," translates into the adult attitude, "If it's good for me, then I'll try to make it good for the company. But if I can't, then at least it's still good for me. And that's okay."

A while back, one of the nation's leading packaged goods companies was recruiting at a top business school. One of the candidates interviewing for a marketing position asked the question, "As I work for your company, where will I need to put my effort—in competing against your largest competitor, or against the person in the office next to me?"

The candidate was surprised by the answer, not so much by what was said, but by the immediate candor in which it was given: "Well," said the interviewer, "there will come a time when there will be one position available for multiple candidates. It's up to you to be sure you look better than the others." This flew in the face of the candidate's belief, perhaps overly innocent, that if you put the success of the company first, even if it means empowering and improving others, you'll be recognized for your contribution. Shades of Carla's story told earlier and the golden goose syndrome she faced.

For this company, playing nice and supporting the team was not the road to success. Luckily for the candidate, who went on to create a new national presence for another employer that dominated its industry, he found out the fit was wrong before he took the job.

There is only so much energy you can use; the disposable visionary wants to use it to compete with other companies. PAR employees recognize, perhaps with astute intelligence, that they want to save their energy for fighting inside battles. PARs also tend to have learned the lessons and benefits of risk-aversion. They do what they are told, get the projects done, avoid pushing the envelope, and get satisfactory job performance ratings.

On the other hand, disposable visionaries still seek to dream those childlike dreams that anything is possible and that unorthodox dreams are worth pursuing. They start with instructions but think outside of the box. But pushing boundaries requires strength and desire. It is a childlike pursuit that can be squelched over time. Like many abilities of our youth, it must also be exercised if it is to grow and develop.

As we learned from the CEB research, employees will pursue the path that seems to make the most sense for them personally. The DVS employee has the broadest view of where the company could go but has a narrow, almost blind view of the internal politics of the company. In fact, there are some things the disposable visionary may not see at all, such as the writing on the wall, what is between the lines, what is behind the words of management, and the real rules of the game. Combine this with the childhood tenet of "follow your dreams and trust others," and it's clear why DVS employees are not only blind-sighted at times, but often blind-sided as well.

It's also clear why PAR employees are content to keep a narrow focus and hold their trust very close to their cubicles.

THE WHY

The second aspect of a business brain involves the involuntary functions. These are innate levels of conscientiousness that drive us forward, create our motives, and give us the passion for life. However, the disposable visionary's concept of what defines existence differs greatly from that of the PAR employee.

For the DVS employee, life involves a persistence to achieve. Life ceases when striving ends. The greatest fear is not trying, and it reflects a personal belief that we can continually slay giants. For the PAR employee, life means employment. The greatest fear is doing something to threaten that security.

DVS employees innately believe in their ability to make things happen. Their brains tell them that great things are possible and that obstacles are meant to be overcome, not avoided. They have an inner drive to find a way to slay the beast that is preventing the company from taking a preemptive stand in the marketplace. They think, "Why continue to put out fires when we can create a firewall process that prevents internal issues and ensures customer loyalty?" If it is the right thing to do and if it can be done, then the DVS employee will instinctively search for a way to do it.

Disposable visionaries are driven with a passion to pursue the giant. PARs, on the other hand, may see obstacles as too troublesome or settle for lesser giants. Whereas all employees have drive and want to achieve, PARs tend to have lower standards, and often—too often—management rewards these lesser efforts.

But employees can't slay giants if they're always looking over their shoulders. The beanstalk can't support climbers who are fighting each other for position to get to the top first, or who are undermining those ahead of them. Worse yet, a visionary can't stimulate other climbers to reach for the clouds if the group on the ground sees his beanstalk as a weed and begins to cut it down.

The political function of the brain determines the level of self-promotion and self-recognition. It determines how self-serving an individual is. It is an internal scale weighing the issues of "Do I support myself or others?" "Do I care more about my personal success or the success of the company?" and "At the conclusion of an assignment, do I get the recognition for my contribution, or do I promote the recognition of others?"

The combination of conscientiousness and vision drive a predisposition for passion and meaning that is seldom fueled from the outside. Only 13 percent of employees strongly agree that their job goals will allow them to maximize their full potential, according to Leadership IQ.[7] Conscientiousness and vision are the soul of the disposable visionary. For them, pursuing anything less results in emptiness and discouragement. While some employees may fulfill their needs for passion and meaning through outside activities, the disposable visionary finds fulfillment in applying conscientiousness and vision to her or his daily corporate life.

Look at the diagram of the PAR brain, and you'll that see political sensitivity dominates, which in turn diminishes the importance of vision and conscientiousness: the WAY and the WHY. It's difficult to believe in bigger achievements—which require sharing credit, encouraging others, building a team, and treating others with respect—while simultaneously looking for opportunities to promote yourself over others. The reverse is also true. The stronger the conscientiousness and vision of an employee, the harder it is for the political side to dominate.

This combination of conscientiousness and vision can also affect how employees work together in matrix organizations. Only those who place the organization's vision over their own will continually seek out the input, ideas, and even criticism of others. They recognize the need of others to pursue the greatest opportunities. Ego can be secondary. For the DVS employee, there is little, if any, pride of ownership, except in championing an idea. It doesn't matter who gets the credit, as long as it gets done. But this attitude toward positive change challenges the status quo and, by association, management. That is not always a good thing in a highly political environment or in one that is averse to boat-rockers.

For the PAR employee, political sensitivity rules the day. Almost every decision is based on how it affects oneself vs. those things bigger than ourselves. In the PAR employee, its function is primarily to carry out a long-established credo: *Conceitus, ergo sum*, or "I promote myself, therefore I stick around."

THE WHOA

Political skill, combined with the amygdala's fight-or-flight response, determines the WHOA—the sense of when to move forward and when to back off. Just as the physical brain instinctively prevents the body from pain or adjusts appropriately in different environments, so too the corporate brain provides warning signs to protect our well-being.

Times always arise when decisions have to be made whether to proceed or not. In a corporate environment, these decisions may reflect how we view the culture, the politics, our role, and our individual risk-reward values. Political skill dictates how employees understand and adjust to the culture in which they work. It helps employees to assess the environment and gives them one last opportunity to wait before they act. For PAR employees, political skill helps to protect their jobs. For others . . . well that's why Disposable Visionary Syndrome can often become a terminal condition.

Our body is blessed with a gag reflex, which prevents us from choking on things that just aren't natural for us to swallow. In the same way, the professional brain offers a cultural or political reflex that carefully assesses the degree to which the "apparent sincerity" of a boss or coworker matches his or her actions. It reflects an individual's capacity to understand, process, and deal with corporate politics. In the PAR brain, it carefully weighs options and effectively evaluates possible actions. In the DVS brain, it is less effective, processing politics as it would any other potentially hazardous element: It takes very small bites or simply rejects them completely. Political skill is compressed in the DVS brain. There can be little room for political consideration when the brain is driven by vision and a focus on eventual achievement of what matters.

PAR employees have become conditioned over time to respond immediately to key stimuli in a politically astute and risk-averse manner. Over time, responses are second nature and no longer require a process to weigh options, instead sending a fight-or-flight signal to the spine, also known as "corporate backbone."

When PAR employees hear, "Now go work as a team," their brains carefully process it and immediately communicate, "Lay low, and wait for the opportunity to look good or to add enough doubt to the process that nothing gets done."

A normal meeting of traditional (PAR) employees: A collection of the disengaged, chosen by the unmotivated, to do the unimportant.

Corporate politics can be the great warning sign in a company. It seldom offers permission to proceed at full speed. Those who can accept and understand it know when to proceed with caution and when to yield to others. PAR employees have a finely tuned brain in this area, evolved over years of use. And the more they use it, the more they become comfortable with and comforted by it. Disposable visionaries would rather not fall prey to its addiction.

Political skill determines how well we adjust and conform to our environment, and in particular it relies heavily on the concept of "apparent sincerity." This ability to absolutely convince others of one's good intentions, regardless of results, gives practitioners the ability to blend in, and it is especially active after a mistake or perceived political blunder. It allows the individual to look like all the other employees. There is nothing that particularly stands out as superior, but there also isn't anything that detracts or looks inferior. It is perfect corporate camouflage. Nothing is provided that will catapult the company forward, but there is also nothing that will catapult the employee out the window. At the very least, it allows the PAR to mimic the Mediocrat, and it keeps the boat moving.

For the DVS employee, no such camouflaging function is available, so the brain has evolved to provide another ability: resilience in the face of obstacles. Rather than blending in, it enables the employee to rebound. Following political or internal defeats, the DVS employee is still driven by the vision, still obsessed by what could be. So the disposable visionary's resilience develops into a source of balance and stability. It explains how she can keep standing while rocking the boat, how she can maintain the vision while the sea tosses her. And it also explains why, even if thrown overboard by the row-master or her galley mates rather than the elements, she is ready to do the same thing on the next boat that offers an opportunity.

From the corporate pressures and individual responses, a natural consequence has developed: a desire for survival. In all employees, there are some basic desires: all appreciate recognition, all value some stability, and all want to eat. For the DVS employee, the brain believes that doing whatever creates the greatest positive impact for the customer and the company—immediately and in the long run—will provide those benefits. Carla certainly believed that. For the PAR employee, these desires are also strong, but they take on a focus that self-promotion and excelling at the corporate game has greater potential.

An examination of the brain functions explains why DVS employees can be so attuned to the big picture yet miss those things that others would consider commonsensical for survival. It also explains why DVS employees are puzzled by how others seem to miss the big picture and concentrate on the trivial.

The different functional priorities of DVS and PAR brains should come as no surprise. For over a century, medical science has identified that there is a left brain and a right brain. A popular theory has attributed each side with its own functions and dominance in different individuals. Those who are more comfortable with one type of brain are uncomfortable and usually don't easily understand those with tendencies from the other side. In corporate cultures that do not grasp or appreciate the functions of the DVS brain, these employees do not last very long. In hindsight, the manager will often realize—usually too late—that these employees brought a refreshing approach to vision, teamwork, and passion. In other words, functions of the DVS brains were indeed right. And those employees with less drive, less initiative, and less passion are usually those that are left.

In summary, disposable visionaries don't worry about gray matter or white matter. They just focus on what matters.

So, what does this mean?

As a visionary, you are driven to achieve. Your brain is geared toward identifying and pursuing things of impact. Not everyone, including your peers and managers, may share this perception of what is important. But you must do what you were designed to do: reflect what drives and excites you as an individual. At the same time, realize that the actions and attitudes of others may also be ingrained and not easily attuned to pursuing the big picture.

BILLY MITCHELL

WHY THE U.S. AIR FORCE ALMOST WASN'T

Billy Mitchell was born into a military family, enlisted for service in the Spanish-American War, and quickly became a lieutenant in the army. After attending the Army Staff College and serving on the Mexican border, he secured an assignment on the General Staff in 1912. He could have enjoyed this coveted staff post, but he resigned from it in 1915 to enroll in flight school. This led to his command of the first and largest use of air power in a military engagement. He concluded his mission in World War I with the rank of brigadier general.

By most accounts, Mitchell could have enjoyed a high rank in the military, but he was driven by his passion to legitimize the airplane as a military weapon. And this led to his conflict and eventual dismissal from the military.

Mitchell had two key visions for military air power: the first was simply to obtain the funding and support for air power development. The existing military was prejudiced toward traditional naval and infantry warfare and viewed the airplane primarily as a surveillance tool. To maximize the potential of military air power, Mitchell also advocated a unified control of military air power, rather than splitting control among the services.

Mitchell angered the military establishment by proving the potential of air power. He secretly increased his company's bomb capacity in a successful postwar demonstration sinking the captured German battleship *Ostfriesland,* which many thought unsinkable. While his action frustrated his superiors' self-serving agenda, it also spurred the navy to conduct further tests during 1923, the results of which initiated the navy's development of the aircraft carrier as an offensive weapon.

While Mitchell's efforts proved his point, his lack of conformity to the military line and his relentless devotion to push for the creation of an independent air force angered his superiors and resulted in his demotion to colonel and assignment to the VII Corps Area in San Antonio. His continued outspokenness led to an accusation of insubordination. He was convicted in a court-martial and sentenced to five years' suspension in 1926. Rather than accepting this suspension for an eventual retirement, Mitchell resigned his commission and continued a public campaign for his beliefs.

In hindsight, almost all of Mitchell's theories about the role of air power in warfare proved true—including a remarkable, and much scoffed-at, assessment that the navy's fleet at Pearl Harbor was vulnerable to carrier-launched air attack . . . and that the attack would be made by Japan.

After his death, his positions were vindicated, and he is now considered the father of the U.S. Air Force. His memory was further honored, ironically, when the military named the WWII B-25 bomber for him: the Mitchell Bomber.[8]

Chapter 4

The Disposable Visionary/ Management Dictionary

The curse of actually believing what you hear

I know you understand what you think I said, but I'm not sure that you realize that what you heard is not what I meant.

Richard Nixon

The disposable visionary employee looks at things from a vision of "what could be." The PAR employee looks at things from a vision of "what I'd better watch out for." The former looks for potential. The latter looks for potholes. One looks for light, the other for limits.

This might explain how each takes instructions or management statements and runs in a different direction. They hear things with a different filter and thus interpret words and instructions differently. As such, it might be appropriate to provide an employee–management dictionary, defining this individual interpretation (Table 4.1).

Table 4.1   The DVS/Management Dictionary

What management says:	What management usually means:	What DVS employees think:	What most PAR employees think:
Tell me what you think	*Tell me how to tweak this, but don't change anything substantial*	*They really want me to tell them what I think and how to make it better*	*I need to make a few comments to get noticed, but nothing that would require more work, especially from my area*
Let's think out of the box	*Don't you dare think out of the box—we don't want a revolution*	*They want a revolution*	*They want us to come back with the same stuff, just with different words*
We want you to change the culture	*We're supposed to be open to change, but let's not get crazy*	*They want me to get crazy*	*They are looking for scapegoats. Culture is not my job, and they don't want it to be my job*
Hey, how's it going?	*Just tell me everything is okay, and let's get on with it*	*They want to know the problems we're having and how to deal with them*	*I need to let them know that there are no problems*
Anything I can help with?	*There isn't anything I need to do, is there?*	*This is a chance to bring up new ideas and get help with new initiatives*	*They're looking for potential problems; never admit you have potential problems*
I'm looking for a volunteer	*I'm looking for a scapegoat*	*They're looking for a hero*	*They're looking for a dweeb to do more work*
We're forming a committee	*We're not sure what we're looking for*	*They're looking to make changes*	*They're looking for lots of dweebs to do more work*
We're looking to reorganize	*We're looking to cut people*	*There's an opportunity to focus on what matters*	*There's a need to look real busy*
We've got a problem	*Well, it's caught up to us again*	*We need to fix the issue once and for all*	*We need a quick answer and to get back to business as usual*
We've got that problem again	*We're having trouble covering this up*	*They need to listen to me*	*They keep listening to me; this is job security*

We're behind you 110 percent	We're going to make changes, but don't go anywhere until we make them	They're committed to improvements	I need to lie low and get to know the boss better
We need to increase profitability	We need to cut people	They need dramatic ways to increase revenue or improve efficiency	I need to find something to do that my boss doesn't understand
We want to improve our people	We don't want to spend a lot on training and development	I need to propose ways to stretch our thinking and impact	I need to show them that they don't need to spend any money on me
We'll take it under advisement	We'll ditch it	They'll look at and get back to me; I'll continue to work on improving it	I'm glad I didn't spend my time on that
We're not sure you're a team player	You're outta here	They're evaluating how we can make greater contributions	I need to say yes more often
We're looking for new opportunities for you	You're outta here	They are finally looking at places we can kick butt	I've got to protect my butt
That's not the way we've usually done things around here	That is really *not* the way we *ever* want to do things around here	They need time to get used to the idea	I'll never mention that again
We don't have politics here	Of course we have politics here	I can focus on getting things done and not worry about politics	There are some major *political* landmines here
We question your judgment	We question your political savvy	What did I do wrong?	I need to find an inside supporter . . . or an outside lawyer
We really want to step up	We want progress but not change	The sky's the limit: we need to look for where the company can really go and take steps to get there	I'll step back and watch for where they're serious before I take any steps

We hear things the way we are predisposed to hear them. The DVS brain works differently. The DVS employee has a different way of hearing things. He trusts those who lead the company. He takes things at face value and presses on to make a difference. He doesn't take the time to look at what is behind the words. He doesn't have the capacity, time, or interest to look at the political implications behind management statements. So while others are puzzled by why the DVS employee didn't see the writing on the wall or hear what others feel are obvious hints, the DVS employee looks for the opportunities to continue his quest for corporate, not personal, improvement. He looks for opportunities to make a difference and grabs onto any permission to do so—perhaps with the wrong dedication and at the wrong time. But to him, there is no wrong time for improvement.

Does management purposely mislead by its words? No. Often, they see the underlying message as being very clear. Very often, they don't know the whole story themselves, so their words of direction or encouragement might disguise or filter what is really going on. But the DVS employee will look for the opportunities that allow him to drive to ways that make a difference, just as the PAR employee reads into messages with his own interpretation.

So the DVS employee presses on, looking for the chance to enhance, improve, and impact the organization and its processes. To a less driven manager, this pushing can be perceived like a child who keeps asking for candy. Pushing and pushing gets tiring after awhile. Except the DVS employee is not seeking treats, only permission.

When managers take much of their time to deal with the day-to-day issues, they get bothered by DVS staff who push on the greater opportunities. They can become the squeaky wheel or the constant itch. As managers are pressed, they begin to feel uncomfortable. And when we itch, we scratch. Unfortunately, the disposable visionary's persistent desire to push and question only creates more itching, until their boss is tired of admitting ignorance or just of dealing with what is perceived as an irritant. Of course, when you remove the irritation, the itching stops—but unfortunately, so do the questions and the opportunities for enhancement.

The good and bad thing about a squeaky wheel is that it gets our attention. It is supposed to get our attention. But it is a lot of work to take it off, examine it, oil it, repair it, and reset it, especially if your mind is on other, presumably more pressing issues. It's also a lot of work to stop and check the other wheels too, to see if they might be weak and need repair or replacing. It's funny: the squeaky wheel is the one we complain about. It implies that the wagon isn't operating smoothly. But often the squeaky wheel is carrying the most weight. That is why it squeaks. But looking objectively at all the wheels takes a lot of time when you're trying to get to market and you're tired of people looking up when they hear the squeaks. But the merchant has to get his goods to market, so in the short term, it seems easier just to take it off than to try to fix it. But later, he wonders why it's so hard to get anywhere with only three—albeit identical—wheels.

"Hi Meredith. I'd like your suggestions on how we can do things faster with fewer people and a smaller budget. But don't change the way we do things."

The following is an example of how a squeaky wheel was not just eliminated but actually changed the way it sounded. Even though this particular company's stated objective was to become more efficient and productive, it quickly changed direction once the implications became clear.

WHEN TOTAL QUALITY DIDN'T TOTAL UP

In the 1990s there was huge emphasis on companies to have a total quality management (TQM) system in place.[1] Total quality management is a process by which a company continually evaluates and improves its product quality. It requires a complete buy-in by all employees, since quality improvement is a daily effort and since finding problems or opportunities can take place anywhere on the line or throughout the company. One of the nation's largest direct marketing companies was told by its largest client that it needed to present its TQM credentials if they were continue working together. The company brought all of its employees together for a "Quality

Kick-Off" and told them, "For the next four months, we will turn this company upside down, assessing our current operations, identifying how we can work together to meet new standards, and putting key new initiatives and measurements in place to ensure that we are constantly looking for new ways to improve our operations."

A TQM assessment company was brought in to manage the process, set up regular employee meetings to stimulate insights and suggestions, and launched an employee survey on the company's culture, leadership, and employee engagement. The results slammed the company. Seeing the report, the CEO fired the assessment firm and told its internal research director to restate the results in a more positive light. The process was over. The meetings stopped. Employees were cut off. In essence, the company simply declared it had achieved a TQM and moved on. Management had good intentions when it first stated its commitment to change, but what it said it would do and its unwillingness to accept all the consequences resulted in a dramatic shift between what was presented and what became reality. Within ten years, the agency filed for bankruptcy and closed its doors.

CHANGE IS NEVER EASY, BUT IT IS ESPECIALLY HARD ON UNCOMMITTED LEADERSHIP

The Traditional Model

How employees react when given a change opportunity

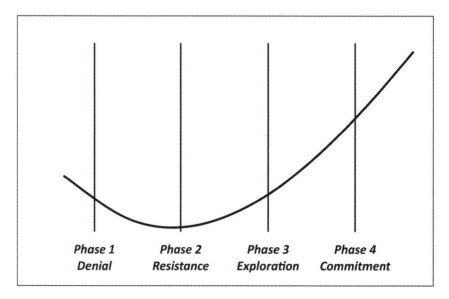

Phase 1	Phase 2	Phase 3	Phase 4
Denial	Resistance	Exploration	Commitment

The Resistant Management Model

How management actually executes a change opportunity

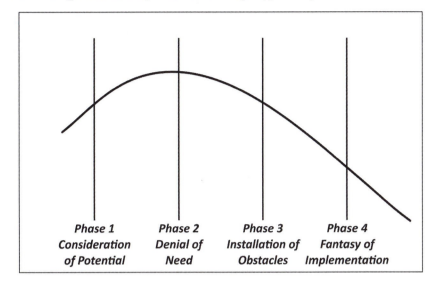

Phase 1	Phase 2	Phase 3	Phase 4
Consideration of Potential	*Denial of Need*	*Installation of Obstacles*	*Fantasy of Implementation*

In a different light, a large medical professional association truly wanted to assess its membership's perceptions of its performance and identify ways to increase its value. After getting high scores on how satisfied its membership was with the association, they decided to measure how indispensable they were to their members' success and whether they were not only meeting but also exceeding their expectations. Instead of their normal satisfaction scores in the seventies and eighties, they got indispensability scores in the teens. However, they were told to prepare for this, since members will rate more harshly on the things that are most important to them and on which they have very specific expectations. Based on these results, the association leadership shared these results with their board, stating up front that the results would be shocking, but then provided a plan of how they would change programs, enhance communications, and adjust their organizational structure to serve members in the areas most important to them. The result was double-digit membership growth.

Perhaps if the marketing agency referenced earlier had been prepared for what to expect from TQM, they would have been more willing to commit to their initial words. Without this warning, they were blindsided and panicked. While their words were superficial, the end spoke for itself.

So, what does this mean?

Get clarity on the mission, vision, and specific expectations, and then use this to filter what you hear and what you think it means. DVS employees want to take the ball and run, but be sure you are playing the same game. By using the corporate vision as the standard, you'll ensure that you are moving in the appropriate direction. If you can clarify what you hear vis-à-vis the vision, you can move management to a new level of performance built on top of its own corporate platform. The truth can be hard to swallow, and it can result in shifting commitments. As you develop new ideas and as the potential implications become clear, be sure to surface them to prevent surprises. However, always present the upside to change, along with the challenge.

THE SMOTHERS BROTHERS

THE NETWORK COULDN'T HANDLE A VISIONARY SHOW, NO MATTER HOW SUCCESSFUL

They started out in television as the sacrificial lamb. Sunday night at 9:00 was a deathblow for any new show—*Bonanza* was more than just dominant; it was lethal, and nine shows on CBS had already fallen in that time slot. So there seemed little to lose when the programming executive chose this seemingly noncontroversial, family-oriented brother act for a four-week run starting February 2, 1967. No one expected it to become the first show to win this slot against the NBC juggernaut. And none expected that the reason for its success would also be the reason its stars eventually got fired while the show was still ranked in the top ten.

In business or entertainment, the formula for success is the same: Know what you can do well, and constantly see how it can be adjusted to meet the needs of your audience, especially when those needs are in flux. It's how some programs stay fresh for years and why some die quickly.

The brothers Smothers knew what made them successful—they took the folk-song genre and twisted it into a comedy format, playing off the traditional with a fresh complement of contemporary, off-beat humor. *The Smothers Brothers Comedy Hour* was clean humor, but it was certainly irreverent to the genre.

What the network expected was a continuation of soft, clean folk-song comedy. What they got was what the brothers always offered: irreverence to a genre, but this time it was to the variety show format. And it worked beyond expectations.

They had a keen sense of the pulse of a dynamic audience in the late sixties. They hired young writers who would be the epitome of successful, countercultural, cutting-edge humor, including Steve Martin, Rob Reiner, Chevy Chase, Bob Einstein, and Pat Paulsen. They brilliantly bridged the generation gap with diverse performers on the same show—the establishment with the revolutionists, such as Kate Smith with Simon and Garfunkel or Jimmy Durante with Janis Ian.

They enjoyed quick success in their time slot in the first year, as CBS gave Tommy Smothers complete creative control. Management figured they had nothing to lose. But as the show openly challenged political policy and took direct shots at the Johnson administration in the second year, network censors became more worried and more aggressive, trimming scripts or cutting entire skits based on their fear of offending conservative audiences. The numbers proved an acceptance by the audience, especially the coveted 15- to 25-year-old segment. But management would not or could not accept the radical push, and even as the show retained its leadership and one month after it was renewed for a fourth season, the boys were fired.

The official reason was based on technicalities, stating that the shows were not delivered on time for pre-air review. Later, it was CBS who was found guilty of breach of contract. But after three years and seventy-three episodes, the Smothers Brothers' only real crime was delivering a show that dramatically changed American television while conflicting with a network management that put politics in its truest sense over performance.

Not only did they predate *All in the Family* (1971), *Saturday Night Live* (1975), and *The Simpsons* (1989), but also without the Smothers Brothers' vision and persistence, those other shows might never have surfaced at all.[2]

Chapter 5

How to Know If You Have Disposable Visionary Syndrome (DVS)

What it is and what it is not

Be wiser than other people if you can; but do not tell them so.

Lord Chesterfield

If you see the humor in what you have read so far, you might have Disposable Visionary Syndrome. If you also feel the pain from some of these situations and pity those who don't, then the chances are even better that you have DVS. You can say, "I've thought that," or "I've been there." You laugh and cry at the same time when considering the examples.

DVS characteristics are reflected in how you regard others, including your staff, peers, and supervisors. They also involve how you look at opportunities, potential, and even setbacks. If you have DVS, you probably can identify with most of the following:

- You are under 40 and have been fired at least twice.
- You feel that all of the firings were unjustified.
- You feel confident that, given the same situation, you would still perform in the same way you did in your previous jobs.
- You tend to take management at their word.

- You envision the potential; you visualize the possibilities and pursue the opportunities that will make your company and your customers more successful.
- You like to work with others, and in fact you appreciate the opinions and insights of others if they provide useful and challenging input.
- You find that most of the time, coworkers do not provide useful and challenging input, but spend too much time complaining or rambling.
- You spend at least half of your time trying to improve the focus, process, approach, service, or products of your company, even if it has to be done in addition to you daily tasks.
- You ask yourself, almost daily, "Why don't they get it?"
- You recognize that you might be a perfectionist, and as such you recognize that you can't always be a perfectionist and still make the impact you want.
- You really don't care what office you have.
- You feel that politics are the opium of business.
- You ask, "Why can't we . . ." at least weekly.
- You work long hours and would expect others to work long hours.
- You really don't care where you park your car.
- You think the best parking places should go to clients and customers and not to management.
- You feel that all information should be open to employees.
- You feel that all employees and their activities should be above reproach.
- You feel that there is always a way to make something better.
- You see the title "maverick" as a compliment.
- You admire not only those who do things better, but also those who do the right things and for the right reasons.
- You recognize the difference between breaking the rules and excelling within the rules.
- You recognize that anyone can make a cheap shot or go for the cheap laugh by using crude or attention-getting gimmicks. The real challenge is to avoid the easy hit and go for the quality.
- You recognize that things that matter will last.
- You throw out conventional wisdom in your quest for what others can't conceive.
- You don't worry about getting fired if you are doing the right things.
- You believe that integrity matters.
- Your focus is on beating the competition and not on beating your coworkers.

- You believe that your company really wants people who can make an impact for the company and for your customers.
- You'll give up the raise if it means that more people can stay at work to get the company over the next hump.
- You never consider race, sex, or age in looking for input or considering the opinions of others.
- You feel both justification and sadness when you see your previous employer struggle after you leave.
- You now understand that culture is more important than your immediate boss when looking at your next employer.
- In spite of obvious instruction or mentorship, you still refuse to stoop to self-promotion.
- You have difficulty saying "I" and usually refer to "We," even if you did most of the work.
- You feel that if no one else is going to take leadership, you will.
- You realize that to be successful, a company has to appeal to the emotional as well as the intellectual.
- You know that impact can be created through attention to detail as well as attention to the bigger picture, as long as a breakthrough vision is set for both.
- You recognize that working smarter instead of harder requires a clear vision and permission.
- Having the freedom to excel is more important than getting a reward for maintaining the status quo.
- You don't believe in the status quo.
- You take pleasure in attempting what others quickly say can't be done.
- You take pleasure in seeing others grow and become successful in building up your ideas.
- You have little pride of authorship.
- You don't want to make your boss or anyone look bad.
- Without thinking about it, you actually want to make your boss look good by focusing on what can really matter to the customer and the organization, not on the political agenda.
- You're not out to make yourself look smart or others look stupid.
- You worry about what others think about your ideas, and so you get their input to make them better, but you don't worry about what others think about you.
- You focus on things that have lasting effect.
- You believe that employees should be devoted to making their company as successful as possible.

- You don't think about how success will prepare you for moving on to another company.
- You understand the difference between rules, restrictions, and obstacles. Rules are to be respected; restrictions are to be questioned; obstacles are to be overcome.
- You realize that others often confuse restrictions and obstacles with rules and don't pursue the possible due to their own shortsightedness.
- You don't avoid conflict on a core idea; in fact, you welcome it, even seek it out, if it will make the end result better.

Those blessed or cursed with DVS exhibit a combination of extremes—that Forrest Gump/Thomas Edison combination we spoke of earlier. Interestingly, both are necessary to produce great things. Unfortunately, they also involve characteristics that can frustrate, challenge, and irritate others.

At one extreme, DVS employees pursue a strong passion for improvement. They are not content with the status quo. They are always searching for what is not only better but also usually the best. There is a strong drive for perfection, not so much obsessed with minor details but rather the big impact. However, as we will discuss later, some DVS employees are focused on how certain details can indeed create a big-picture impact. If a DVS employee were designing a car, he would not be so concerned with what color consumers preferred. He would be questioning why it couldn't it come with a 12-year bumper-to-bumper warranty. Or why can't the owner have an automatic trade-in incentive on the next model so that it preempts the competition from tempting him to consider another make or dealer?

A DVS employee in healthcare would ask, "Why can't we create preventive programs that would ensure 100 percent customer satisfaction?" And truthfully, if given the freedom to pursue that goal, he or she might actually identify the concepts that would achieve it.

In retailing, he would ask and pursue the question, "Why can't we create customers for life, including immediate and extended families?" In financial services, he would propose lifetime mortgages that would follow a customer, rather than requiring a new payoff schedule with each house. He would ask, "If I borrowed $100,000, why can't I keep paying it off if I move?" And he would find the financial model that makes it profitable. In manufacturing, he or she might find new ways to ensure satisfaction guarantees, perhaps combining enhanced service functions with improved quality. Here, making the details work is the key advantage.

In auto insurance, he would develop a phone app that prevents texting while driving but doesn't interfere with passenger texting. This would be tied to lower insurance rates and could generate interest in additional apps that reinforce safe driving habits.

In the retail toy arena, she would be focused on how to attract the grandparent segment, who purchase 25 percent of all toys, away from Walmart and Target. She would do this through exclusive service concepts and alliances with other category giants, such as book or music stores, to provide integrated gift packages that guarantee satisfaction in service and product selection.

Regardless of their position or placement, DVS employees ask the core question, "How can I make my area a competitive advantage?" Whether it is marketing, IT, sales, production, quality control, customer service, human resources, accounting, or facilities management—you name it—that department can become a source of enhanced revenue or reduced cost for the company.

In their pursuit of enhancements, DVS employees seldom take the easy route. They are not employees that settle. If they were joke writers, they wouldn't settle for the cheap gag, the vulgar line, or the dirty joke. They would seek an idea or premise that could launch an entire dialogue that is funny in concept as well as in words. It would take a lot longer to develop, and it might require numerous rewrites and group sessions, but the result would more likely be a classic routine than a throwaway gag.

DVS involves the pursuit of what matters. It looks for opportunity. Often the concept is not fleshed out down to the details, but instead concentrates on an ultimate goal that will change the playing field. As such, the ideas themselves are works in progress that still have the potential for improvement as the program develops.

This is also an important characteristic for the DVS employee: She usually isn't concerned with pride of authorship. Interestingly, while this characteristic may be, on paper, a thing an employer values, in practice employers may not perceive the true value of the DVS employee, since other employees may get or seize recognition for her work.

There are many more characteristics of DVS employees. As the list above indicates, they are focused on the big picture and ways to achieve the greatest opportunities. They recognize the value of others and put the overall good above their own recognition. But their persistent drive can have a tendency to rub others who do not share their values the wrong way. There is often a fine line between DVS employees and other employees who also don't fit, but for different reasons. The DVS employee is outwardly-focused. Some employees who also conflict with others may do so for self-focused reasons. Don't confuse DVS with stubbornness, insensitivity, or stupidity. Employees with these attributes are not DVS employees. They are just jerks.

Employees with the following characteristics do not have Disposable Visionary Syndrome. They just have problems. Even if you think you are right and the rest of the company is wrong, even if you feel that no one listens to your suggestions, even if you think your ideas will help the company, you probably do not have DVS if . . .

- You have a personal agenda that is not in line with the corporate good or the customers' best interests.
- You are driven by personal perfectionism to the point that it gets in the way of the big picture.
- You build personal or departmental silos that do not work effectively with other departments or your peers.
- You would rather do everything yourself or within your own department, without seeking out the advice of others—especially those who have valuable insights, but whom you just don't like.
- You want the credit and recognition for ideas, or you won't pursue them at all.
- You respect the input of others but don't have the time or patience to listen to them.
- You are out to make yourself look smart and, at times, to expose the ignorance or shortsightedness of others.
- You propose lots of ideas, many not thought through at all, to allow others to pick out which to pursue; you want to get labeled as "the idea person," but you aren't passionate about any of the ideas, and you let others determine which to follow.
- You don't want to change the world, just to create a better perception of yourself within the corporation.
- You give up when the politics gets tough.
- You put your passion and desires above integrity.
- You watch others take heat without stepping in.
- You'd rather present a good idea yourself than get help in presenting a great concept taken to a level that addresses the key issues.
- You just like to hear yourself talk.
- You worry about severance before you pursue the completion of your ideas.
- You worry about what others will think about you.
- You think about personal repercussions before you speak your mind about important issues.
- You see all teams as obstacles rather than potential partners.
- You worry about your pension.
- People perceive you as presenting a "my way or the highway" stance.
- You take pride in your stubbornness.
- You take pleasure in just winning for winning's sake.

Many employees may believe that they have an altruistic approach to their business, when actually they seek to promote the company for their own recognition. This is not Disposable Visionary Syndrome. The ego is far supplanted in the DVS employee. They take risks and don't worry about the politics, which is why they are so often fired. These other employees have a greater personal agenda. The DVS employee is seen as compulsive/obsessive. The other type of employee is just compulsive/obnoxious.

The difference is seen when the going gets tough. The self-serving employee backs down. His passion for job preservation supersedes his passion for his idea. The DVS employee continues to fight for what he or she feels has the best potential for the company. The idea and the passion take center stage. And he expects the value of the idea to survive the conflict. The DVS employee believes that it is up to management to see the value of both the idea and the employee. He also trusts that a manager will at least take the time to understand the full impact of the vision and will weigh the value of the idea against the conflict it may create.

Too often, this can be a fatal assumption. But when it is not, it brings breakthrough potential.

So what does this mean?

Disposable Visionary Syndrome is more than just the appearance of being a maverick. True DVS employees recognize the risks as well as the rewards of change and are committed to its achievement. Realize that when the pressure for appearances versus substance is felt, that is when your true colors will come out. Real DVS employees take responsibility for their actions and defend others by staying true to the vision.

DAVID NEELEMAN

TOO REVOLUTIONARY EVEN FOR THE REVOLUTIONARIES

Even an organization publicly praised for its innovation and dedication to the customer can be overwhelmed by the visionary. It happened at Southwest Airlines, and now the departed visionary may eventually become the airline's biggest threat.

David Neeleman is the wunderkind of the airline industry. In 1984, with June Morris, he launched Morris Air. There, he was the one who introduced

(Continued)

the industry's first e-ticketing system and pioneered the use of at-home airline reservationists, cutting overhead and providing greater staffing flexibility. By 1992, he had attracted the attention of Southwest Airlines, which purchased Morris Air, gaining both a West Coast presence and the talent of Neeleman.

Combining Neeleman's talent and insights for strategic airline innovations with Southwest's reputation for customer focus should have resulted in a true dream team. However, Neeleman soon recognized that even a storied company can be resistant to a flurry of new ideas, even when they are perfectly aligned with the vision and mission of the company. Within six months, the "kindred spirits," as Southwest CEO Herb Kelleher initially described them, drew up a non-compete agreement when Neeleman was asked to leave. According to former human resources staff, Neeleman's passion was often delivered with a lack of diplomacy, facing a slower corporate pace. One of the industry's greatest minds and innovators rocked the boat . . . and was shown the door.[1]

However, after his five-year non-compete expired, Neeleman took the same vision and ideas that he tried to implement at Southwest and began a new airline, JetBlue. Based on his passionate belief that even a low-cost airline can rise to a new level of service, Neeleman's airline combined a single-aircraft philosophy (all planes are Airbus A320, allowing more efficient operating and maintenance costs) and low fares, with electronic reserved seating, Web site purchase options, individual 24-channel satellite TV, all-leather interior, all-you-can-eat fun snacks, and superior customer service. Even pilots agreed to help clean an aircraft to enable a quicker turnaround and increase passenger miles and revenue. When Neeleman flew, he also pitched in to clean each plane he was on. In 2002, he donated his entire salary to the JetBlue Crewmember Crisis Fund, which assists JetBlue employees facing financial difficulties.

Neeleman's vision set new standards. In 2002, when the industry lost $6 billion, JetBlue earned $54.9 million, with an operating margin of 16.5 percent—higher than all major airlines and twice Southwest's 7.6 percent.[2,3] In an industry when cost control may be a key to success and even existence, JetBlue's cost per available seat mile was almost half of United's and 14 percent lower than Southwest's, as reported in 2002 fourth-quarter statistics. In March 2001, JetBlue was voted the number-two domestic airline in the Zagat Airline Survey.[4] Forbes magazine dubbed Neeleman the "Lord of the Skies" as his competitive threat continued to climb.[5]

But Disposable Visionary Syndrome can be repetitive. Despite his personal apologies and efforts to resolve complaints, Neeleman was replaced as JetBlue CEO following a 2007 JFK ice storm that left thousands of JetBlue customers stranded on the runway for hours due to weather and traffic grid-lock. However, this firing led to his 2008 creation of Azul Brazilian Airline, which became the first airline in the world to board more than two million passengers in its first year, with the highest load factor in the market at almost 80 percent.[6] Following Neeleman's commitment to champion and lead the concept of low-cost travel with the highest service quality, in 2011 the airline was voted "Best Airline in Brazil" by both *Tourism* and *Flight Revue* magazines, was named "Best Low-Cost Airline in Latin America" by Skytrax, and was recognized by *Advertising Age* as one of the "World's 30 Hottest Brands."[7]

Azul is currently the third largest airline in Brazil. With a fleet of 145 aircraft and over 10,000 crewmembers, the company currently has a 33 percent share of departures of the Brazilian aviation market. In 2014, Azul was named best low cost carrier in Latin America for the fourth consecutive time by Skytrax. The airline was also named best low cost carrier in the world by CAPA in 2012 and is recognized by FlightStats as having the best on-time perfor-mance in Latin America.

Ever the innovator, Neeleman led the industry in new fuel ventures in 2012 as well when Azul partnered with Amyris, Inc., Embraer, and GE, pioneering a demonstration flight using a renewable jet fuel made from Brazilian sugar cane, which a study indicated could reduce greenhouse gas emissions up to 82 percent vs. conventional jet fuel.[8]

The vision continues.

Chapter 6

The Four Styles of DVS
There is diversity even among revolutionaries

Every calling is great when greatly pursued.

Oliver Wendell Holmes Jr.

As we have mentioned, there are common characteristics among DVS employees, besides finding themselves looking for employment on numerous occasions. They all are visionaries. They all are dreamers. They all seek improvement and things that have potential for the greatest impact. They all trust that things can get done if allowed to proceed. They all ask, "Why are we wasting time doing this, when we could be doing something that dramatically improves the way we do business or the way we serve our customers?" They all take opportunities to heart.

However, even among DVS employees, there are differences. As with people in general, they have individual strengths, preferences, and tendencies. Among visionaries, some are more conceptual, more big picture, more artistic and more intuitive. And there are also those who are more detailed, more communicative and more pragmatic. While they all seek dramatic new opportunities and take them to heart, each might do so with a different focus.

One thing about DVS employees is they are not limited to a common perception or approach to enhanced vision. So, with different ways to affect change, visionaries tend to fall into five different styles (see Figure 6.1). These reflect their comfort or tendencies that might be condensed onto two axes. Each axis is a visionary scope. The vertical axis reflects the employee's focus on how to enhance the company. It is the **What** that can be dramatically improved or enhanced to enable the company to compete more effectively. It's a directional vision that formulates where the company needs to go or what it should do.

The horizontal axis concerns improvements on **How** the company might achieve new impact. It is more of an executional vision that focuses on the most effective means to get there. It centers on how to engage others, or how to create a culture that is more diligent or excited to perform at a new level.

On the vertical Corporate Enhancement axis—the **What**—some visionaries tend to concentrate on ways to revolutionize based on the big picture: new programs, new innovations, new positioning, new services, or new directions. Other visionaries tend to create impact with a vision that revolutionizes the details: new ways of doing things, how to get greater efficiency, how to cut costs. Both styles require breakthrough approaches for the maximum results. Both look at what could be and are not constrained by the status quo.

The horizontal Engaging Others axis reflects a people orientation. Some visionaries get others involved by actions: identifying new ways to get people involved, developing teams or new organizational structures that enhance performance. Others focus more on new ways to build and leverage people's emotions: getting them excited and passionate about the vision and stimulating their ideas and mental involvement.

If we were to use these two dimensions for segmentation, we would find four core segments . . . and a fifth, middle segment, identifying a generalist DVS who touches on all four profiles.

Each style of visionary rocks the boat in his or her own special way. No single style has a greater impact than the others. For some organizations, finding a way to decrease costs by 20 percent is more impactful than increasing sales 30 percent. Finding an effective way to finally put out the constant fires enables others to pursue new opportunities. Thus, having a variety of visionary employees with various styles in various roles and departments can result in an influx of improvements: all on things that matter, and all with the potential to provide powerful enhancements.

Each visionary style offers a different perspective on and approach to organizational improvement. And each faces its own special resistance.

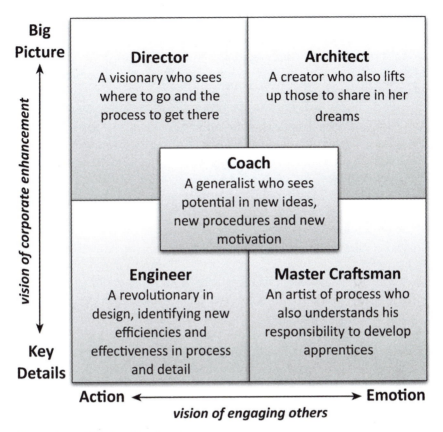

Figure 6.1   DVS Profile Chart

The Director/Orchestrator: This visionary type is tuned into identifying new directions, enhanced vision, and company-focus opportunities. She also is attuned to orchestrating the pieces to get it done: how to organize the organization, how to get more things done that matter, or identifying the internal obstacles.

Because these ideas often come with recommended organizational change and impact, the Director's ideas are often perceived as more detailed than they really are. The T's and I's are not usually crossed and dotted, but because she is only able to talk about some of the organizational issues, she can make an opportunity seem complicated to implement—even though it is the organizational impact that may actually bring the greatest opportunity. In fact, that is often disposable visionary's downfall: if she presents big-picture potential and also presents organizational opportunities, she may overwhelm her audience if it focuses more on the obstacles to change than on the opportunities of progress. In this way, her presentation of a dual vision can muddle the story of the big idea. But to those who are open to change, this style enables a company to see not only what is possible but also the initial steps to get there.

DVS employees with the Director style might ask such questions or seek out opportunities such as . . .

- How can we focus our energies on what matters?
- What internal alignment will allow us to get there more effectively?
- What major political issues may prevent us from focusing on the big opportunities?
- How can we integrate the departments to work more effectively to create programs, products, and services that really matter to the company and our customers?
- Why can't we make each department become a competitive advantage for us?

There is no question that the impact DVS employees bring to an organization is exactly what management wants, or says they want. But real impact requires change. And though management may not be prepared for change, they are usually prepared with ways to deflect the suggestions. Therefore, the DVS Director will also become very familiar with responses such as . . .

- We aren't organized that way.
- That isn't what we're designed to do.
- Do you know what that would entail?
- That's interesting, but . . .
- It sounds too complicated.
- We need something less involving.
- We need something more exciting.
- Just leave it to me, I'll work on it.
- Those areas aren't your concern.

The Engineer/Designer: This DVS style is exhibited in one who likes to make it right. He looks for new ways to get things done that can dramatically help the organization or the customer. He has a nose for improving design, processes, or operations. He asks why things can't be made better, cheaper, or with more efficiency and looks for the revolutions—not simply evolutions—that will achieve it.

The Engineer may be the best source for finding the solutions for the obstacles that the Director/Orchestrator identified. The Engineer is driven by the potential that comes from pursuing opportunities by seeking answers to questions such as . . .

- How can we operate more efficiently in striving to achieve our corporate mission?
- What operational issues are getting in the way?
- What processes are keeping each department from becoming a competitive advantage.
- What processes are not perceived as important to the customer?
- What are we doing that we can change to become better, faster, or cheaper?
- What are we doing that is not directly impacting what is really important to the customer?
- What are we doing that is wasting people's time?

The Engineer also meets internal walls that derail his potential. This style meets some of the heaviest political roadblocks, since any process impacts all or most areas in a company. His ideas and innovations are often met with verbal roadblocks such as . . .

- Let's meet on that someday.
- We'll need to get a committee together to discuss that.
- We'll need a process to evaluate that.
- We need growth strategies, not process ideas.
- We're too overextended to take the time to consider improving efficiency.
- We just learned this process. We aren't going to change anything now.
- That may be a lot of work to only impact a few people.
- That may be a lot of work since it impacts so many people.
- I can't take the time to explain why this won't work. It's too complicated.
- That would step on too many toes.
- We can't control most of the other departments.

The Architect/Creator: This style is always looking at the big picture in a way that motivates the heart—looking at the dramatic opportunities that will excite both employees and customers. This style might be well described as that of an architect: creating a dynamic building that incorporates the personal needs of its tenants as well as the visual appeal that would not only get tenants' interest, but also would be sensitive to and gain the necessary approval of the city council or board of development.

This is a broad yet comprehensive style. As this style of visionary observes what is going on and the opportunities for growth and enhancement, he or she might ask . . .

- What can we do that can dramatically improve how we serve our customers?

- How can we focus on becoming indispensable to our customers?
- What are the new ways we can fulfill our corporate mission and meet new customer needs?
- How are customer needs stretching our corporate mission, and can we successfully respond in a way that preempts the competition?
- How can we serve our customers in such a way that price will never become an issue or a threat?
- How can we get our people excited about doing what really matters?
- How can we align every employee around our vision for greater impact for our customers?
- How do we give each employee the freedom to be passionate about our vision and to seek to contribute in innovative and more productive ways as they see those opportunities on their own?
- What prevents our employees from taking every initiative that would enhance our customers' dependency on our organization?

Of course, when they present solutions to these problems, they are presented themselves with questions and comments such as . . .

- Have you really given it much thought?
- How can you argue with the success we've had?
- We need process ideas, not new strategies.
- We'll address those thoughts after we have today's business in hand.
- That's not our style.
- That's really off the wall.
- We need more detail.
- People need structure to perform.
- What if we gave everyone that kind of freedom?

The Master Craftsman/Engager: This employee tends to look at opportunities to improve the passions of people—to motivate them to constantly improve processes and take pride in their day-to-day activities. He or she is able to motivate with a push strategy that is sensitive to the emotions of people.

The Master Craftsman wants to help people succeed and enjoys a group effort toward visionary improvement of details and processes. The Master Craftsman seeks to add a spark that excites people to see ways of doing things that will enhance the internal and external efforts of the company. She or he will look around and seek solutions to such questions as . . .

- What can every employee do to either improve revenue or reduce cost?

- Why can't every employee take responsibility for meeting our customers' needs?
- What do we do better than anyone else? How can we leverage that? How can we make it even better? What will make our employees passionate about taking this to the next level?
- What are customers asking for that we are saying no to, and how do we ensure that we change to meet those needs every day?
- How is the work of every employee improving our customers' perception of us?
- What prevents our employees from taking every initiative that would enhance the way we do our business every day?
- Imagine what would happen if we could align our employees around a constant focus on how to be more effective in everything they do.
- What are we doing that is wasting people's focus?

As the Master Craftsman DVS develops solutions to these problems and opportunities, he or she also faces new internal obstacles in the form of change and empowerment resistance . . .

- That'll just cause problems.
- That sounds too simple.
- That sounds too complicated.
- That sounds too risky.
- We can't give our customers everything they ask for.
- We know what our customers want.
- Our customers don't really know what they want.
- Our employees already know they have full latitude to respond.
- You can't give employees that much latitude to respond.

Finally, there is the generalist DVS style, or **Coach**. This employee is on the lookout for a variety of impact opportunities, with a focus on whatever it takes to improve. He may be most likely to see the integration opportunities that combine all the styles. He is often labeled as a "change agent," passionate about a variety of changes. While the other styles may take their visions to a defined and maybe detailed level, the generalist is most likely to need the input of others to consolidate his ideas to the fullest potential. He may also be the most commonly fired, since he is more likely to disrupt more areas at a given time than the other styles.

In some form, he will ask all of the questions that the other styles of DVS employees will ask. And he will probably get a mixture of the same responses.

These styles complement each other . . . especially since visionaries are good at working with others who are able to challenge ideas and stick in the discussion until it becomes "right." Therefore in a multi-DVS environment, they will tend to ask and seek out the answers to questions such as "How will this impact another area?" or "What can we leverage from other areas or approaches to make this work as effectively as possible?"

Thus, with a literal boatload of visionaries, one DVS employee could be finding a new direction; one could be identifying a new, more aerodynamic oar design or how the staff could support stronger or more sails; another DVS employee could be increasing efficiency through better coordination of the rowers; and still another DVS style could stimulate the rowers to want to join in the process of improvement while still contributing to the daily tasks at hand in a more passionate manner.

In a summary, the Architect and Director would both look at the direction of the company, seeking dramatic ways to focus the strategy or vision. In imagining what could be, the Creator may also consider how to engage the employees to be more passionate about how to achieve that vision, so that they all develop an attitude of continuous improvement. The Architect would want every employee to be driven to find innovation on a continuous basis. The Director would try to create that vision by also looking at the organizational implications. He would examine and reorganize the departments and increase the interaction and synergy of the organization toward achieving the vision.

The Master Craftsman and Engineer would both focus on improving details that can change the effectiveness of the company, in the operations or processes, or even changing the emphasis on what details are important. In executing the vision of how to involve others, the Engineer would look more at the organizational opportunities, while the Master Craftsman would look at emotional and personal involvement, with the desire to stimulate an attitude of continual personal dedication to taking the initiative to improve at every opportunity employees see.

If they were building a tree house, the Architect and Director would envision a structure of a size small enough to be cost-effective but large enough and with enough play features that the other kids would not only come, but would be so excited to come that they would always bring the tools to help, as well as snacks and drinks for the others. The Engineer and Master Craftsman would take care of building it in such a way that it was between the right trees and strong enough to hold the neighborhood, as well as the parents who were paying for it, and in such a way that the final design would look like the castle or fort that the others envisioned, built to last. The Architect and Craftsman would also consider the special things that get kids excited about the house, such as color and windows that opened and closed, and they would convey the overall design in a manner that made the other kids actually want to come to help. The

Engineer and Director would help organize the other kids so that the right things were done in the right way—the strong kids establish the structure, the smaller kids secure the rungs and the shingles, and the parents test the final strength.

In a business setting, the Architect would identify that a new family van with unique styling that a man would enjoy driving would fit a growing niche. The Master Craftsman would find a way to combine the room of a van with the image of an SUV. The Engineer would ensure that the design could be executed with both safety and lower cost. And the Director would organize the internal teams in a manner that increased efficiency and ensured integration of quality control.

As you can see, DVS employees carry individual perspectives on ways the company can break through to higher levels. They don't always fit a mold, and each has a passion that can irritate management and others who do not share that passion for ongoing improvement and the search for what could be.

As they pursue their passions, the boat gets rocked. Using a rather simplistic illustration, if a company were fortunate enough to enjoy a boatload of DVS employees, consider the potential opportunities and, of course, some potential obstacles that might arise:

"Hey, Sven, how about heading west?" asks the Architect to the Viking leader. "I hear that there's a city there we haven't plundered yet, and the treasure is immense. If we send out a scout to do a little in-market research, I bet we can come up with a way to attack, minimize our losses, and double our ROI—return on invasion."

"Nah, that sounds like too much work. Look, we've never gone to that country before, and besides, we know the way to Plunderville, and how to break down their doors. We know the routine. We show up, they get scared; we get what we can and leave. Now sit down and stop trying to waste our time."

"But haven't you noticed that each time we go, we get less and less treasure and they seem to be getting better at fending us off? And those 'give us one daughter, keep one daughter' redemption coupons just don't seem to be as effective as they used to be. Besides, the crew is getting bored with the same routine and getting tired of having to fight harder for less reward."

"You heard me—we keep with what has worked. Now sit down."

And so they ignore the Architect type and go back to the old strategy and the old location and wonder why there are less gold, fewer crops, and more barriers each time they arrive.

"Hey, Sven," says the Director, "how about putting the left-handed people on one side and the right-handed on the other? That way we can leverage their strongest sides and cut five days off our travel. And it would also enable

us to use the extra time to try a test invasion in another country, as Olav suggested."

"Nah, we like to integrate our teams, so each side is designed equally. That way, we don't have to test our rowers to see if they are right- or left-handed. We also don't have to worry about measurements or feedback. Besides, we like to give seniority to the oldest rowers, so we give them all the window seats. We don't want to move them just because they could do a better job somewhere else. And like I said before, we don't need to find another country. This one will do fine . . . at least until I retire. Now sit down, grab an oar, and make yourself useful."

"Yo, Svenmeister!" yells the Engineer. "We could give all our rowers a rest if we added an extra mast to hold down the sail tighter. Then we could be stronger when we land and maybe get farther inland to find new treasure and maybe fresh cattle to bring home. I still think steak would be better than all that stale pork we're eating."

"Look, the only wood we could use is from the executive dining table in the galley, and as you know, we don't take anything from that table. We're not touching that. Sit down, and don't mention the cattle thing again. It's the third time you brought it up this trip, and I'm tired of your beef."

"Then how about if we change the mast to fiberglass and make the ship lighter and faster?

"Weren't you listening to me? Sit down!"

And finally, the MasterCraftsman begins, "Excuse me, Mr. Ulgafson? I was wondering, since we only use swords in our battles, wouldn't we be more effective if we gave each warrior a greater selection of weapons and strategy? Especially since we now need to scale walls, fight guerilla resistance, and face cavalry, it seems like we might be better off if we lever-aged the speed of our younger men, enabled our engineers to develop siege equipment, and used others as diversions. This way, the men will also be able to more effectively use those weapons they use best and to work within those units that best use their skills—some are incredibly talented with bows, others with maces, and others with spears. They know what we need to do. Can't we just give them the freedom to leverage their individual talents?"

"Look, we used swords when I started with this boat ten years ago, and we'll use them today. Besides, they all went through the same training when they signed up—six months in the field, six months in sword research, and six months in sword production. Besides, I don't know how to lead these men if they try to use anything other than swords.

"And by the way, I didn't ask for your opinions, I don't want your opinions, and I don't need your opinions. Why don't all four of you go down and start peeling potatoes for dinner? And don't bother signing up for the next voyage.

You're disturbing the other rowers with your constant interruptions and stupid ideas."

And so, they continue to attack the same places with the same weapons, using the same strategy. When they get back to port, in addition to the other layoffs due to declining treasure revenue, there are four DVS dismissals. The good thing about the different DVS styles is that human resources can at least report to management that they maintained diversity . . . in their terminations.

"I called this meeting because you are the only employees who have come up with radical new ideas."

So, what does this mean?

Understand your own tendencies and strengths. Find ways to exploit your DVS style while also trying to broaden your impact in the other styles as well. Be careful not to become a bully with your vision or your style. The needs and focus of the company may change based on the situation, as may the preferences of your supervisor. Don't try to force your style at an inappropriate time.

JONATHAN EDWARDS

THEY COULDN'T HANDLE THE TRUTH

One of the principle advantages of having DVS employees is that the organization will hear the truth, whether it can handle it or not. Too often, people prefer the status quo, rather than reaching for a higher standard that, although requiring more effort or focus, will result in higher personal realization and greater benefit for the entire organization.

One occasion came in a small New England church. Its minister is regarded today as one of the important theologians of the past two centuries, if not the most important one. His teachings are today held in the highest esteem. He is credited with beginning what is known as the First Great Awakening in America. Unfortunately, his own church, which had a front-row seat (or pew) for his teaching, could not handle the standards he set for himself and for his church . . . and he was fired.

Edwards was a unique combination of theologian, preacher, historian, and scholar. He constantly challenged his own beliefs. He bridged the Puritan-Calvinist positions of election and free will and searched the writings of people such as Isaac Newton from a spiritual perspective. Some felt that if not for religion, Edwards would have pursued science as his vocation after he obtained his master's degree at the age of 18 from what is now Yale University.

He is known for his fire-and-brimstone sermon "Sinners in the Hands of an Angry God," but his stimulus of the Great Awakening was fueled by his messages of a loving God of mercy. The revival began with youth, who, though more rebellious (premarital pregnancy rates had risen to one in ten), were actually anxious for higher standards and who were also seeking a loving and merciful God and the standards of excellence that Edwards promoted.

Perhaps Edward's most impactful legacy is the movement from "head knowledge" to practical application of the Christian faith, making religion more reflective of the heart than of the head. His desire was to instill in others a passion for what was right, versus what were rites.

He ushered in a worship environment with new, contemporary hymns that replaced the traditional use of psalms. He applied storytelling to sermons. He encouraged higher behavior of his congregations reflecting their faith. In an example of service that he hoped others would pursue, he personally sacrificed what little he had to help others—but only on the condition of anonymity.

He was perhaps America's most powerful writer and speaker. Yet he was so humble that he asked his wife, Sarah, for her comments before anything was made public. And though he lit the spark of the Great Awakening, he fanned the flame by asking George Whitfield, an English evangelist, to come to the region to preach when he saw the movement stalling.

But pride, politics, and resistance to change forced him out of his pulpit. Many in his congregation did not want to be challenged in their faith. They did not want to face the gap between faith and action. In addition, in Edwards's time, most preachers were pampered with special gifts from members of their congregations, but those who gave the most expected special favor. Edwards did not play favorites. He did not regard tenure with special honor. He did not simply offer membership; he required statements of faith. He wanted to offer inclusion to those converted by the Awakening. But congregations—just like management—can hold fast to the past, and those challenged by his changes were threatened and fired him from his pulpit.

He went on to lead a decade-long ministry to Native Americans, despite a history of violence that included the killing of many of his relatives, and later he became president of Princeton University, where he continued to influence the next generation. His writings, vision, and innovations opened a new wave of religious advocacy that still survives today. The results of the Great Awakening, attributed to his dedication and vision, included as many as 50,000 new converts and 150 new churches.

His impact also resulted in an amazing legacy within his family. Setting an example to pursue the highest calling and standards, of his 1,394 known descendants, Edwards's legacy includes 295 college graduates, 13 college presidents, 65 college professors, 3 United States senators, 30 judges, 100 lawyers, 60 physicians, 75 military officers, 100 preachers or missionaries, 60 prominent authors, one vice president of the United States, and over 80 other public officials, including state governors, foreign ministers, and ambassadors.[1,2]

Chapter 7

Getting Alignment on Your Vision
Flip your presentation if you want to flip opinions

Get your facts first, and then you can distort them as much as you please.

Mark Twain

It's exciting to be a change champion. You find a thrill in making a difference. It's invigorating to see breakthroughs and reveal new insights. The only problem is that others can be just as committed to maintaining the status quo.

Consider the following vignettes. They aren't business examples, but they quickly show that even in a non-business setting, most people just don't grasp the opportunity to look at new ideas, accept change, or regard wise counsel.

1. *Do professionals really seek out information for new ideas and breakthroughs?*
   Consider publications specifically written to reach innovative thinkers. In professions that are supposedly known for their thirst for truth and new ideas, about 200,000 academic journals are printed in English each year. The average number of readers per article is five.

2. *Do those in charge grasp the potential of new ideas?*
   When Einstein published his Theory of General Relativity, the *New York Times* editors sent their golfing correspondent to interview him.
3. *Do people quickly grasp the obvious need for change?*
   James Naismith invented basketball in 1891 when he nailed a peach basket to a pole. After each shot, someone climbed a ladder to retrieve the ball. It took 21 years before anyone decided to cut a hole in the bottom of the basket.
4. *Do people break habits despite the obvious?*
   Millions of people still pray to St. Christopher each year for safety, even though he lost his sainthood in 1969.
5. *Are leaders open-minded enough to consider alternatives?*
   Will they change their minds even when faced with dire consequences or breakthrough opportunities?

In multiple records, there is a retelling of a story involving the Roman emperor Tiberius, who ruled from 14 CE to 37 CE. According to the documents, a man approached the emperor with a new invention: unbreakable glass. It dropped and did not shatter. The man thought this would please the emperor, who instead had the man beheaded, one of the more severe penalties for DVS. The reason for his action? The emperor was threatened by the prospect that such a breakthrough would make his gold and silver worthless.

In another political example, in 1958, under Chairman Mao, the Chinese government established a law to kill all sparrows to prevent them from eating rice grain. This was done to secure more food for the Chinese people. They estimated that the rice supply would increase enough to feed 60,000 more people a year for every 1 million sparrows killed. Some of the council members who were more knowledgeable about the impact opposed this law, fearing unintended consequences. But Mao was not open to the objections of his council. If he had listened, he would have learned that, unfortunately, sparrows don't eat rice, but they do eat the locusts that were now free to eat the grain. This led to the Great Chinese Famine in 1958–61, in which 30 million died.

The moral of all these tidbits is that many people—and perhaps especially people in authority—do not have a natural tendency to grasp new ideas. It's no wonder that they may be even less likely to envision the potential of new ideas or the value of input from those who work for them. New ideas often require an openness to change habits, organizational policies, personnel, personal biases and presumptions, and perhaps the basis of power or influence. It certainly requires humility, one of the leadership characteristics Jim Collins described in *Good to Great*.[1] It demands the possibility that previous standards, procedures, and perceptions should be evaluated for change, and at times, drastic change.

MANAGEMENT FOCUSES TOO OFTEN ON SUSTAINING, NOT STIMULATING

In business literature and management guru-speak, the emphasis is often on efficiency, not effectiveness. This is why most leadership checklists include such elements as team-building, empowerment to do the stated job, emotional awareness, conflict resolution, forgiveness, and change management. These concepts are all essential to a smooth-running organization, but they do not encourage employees to rock the boat, push for creative conflict, or question cultural norms. In the absence of any reward for risk-taking, the result will be a continuation and preservation of the present state. Nothing changes if nothing changes. Perhaps that is why, for many, change management is often unofficially perceived as "change prevention" or "minimum change disruption."

No wonder change agents are often overlooked or perceived as irritants. They interfere with the smooth operation of the company. They demand introspection of priorities. They stimulate discomfort.

This type of organizational complacency would irritate Farrah Gray, a self-made millionaire and CEO of Farrah Gray Publishing. Mr. Gray grew up in a single-parent family in the Chicago projects and was recently named one of the most influential black men in America. Honored in 2010 as one of the 40 Game-Changers by the National Urban League, his view of success is summarized by his philosophy, "Comfort is the enemy of achievement."[2]

Management literature focuses so much on how to comfort the disturbed that it fails to stimulate true change by disturbing the comfortable. True achievement, either from the leadership or the grassroots level, can be linked to the ability to shift to this level of thinking.

SO WHAT IS A CHANGE AGENT TO DO?

In a survey conducted by the authors, a key indicator of impending failure to accept new ideas and change was lack of management alignment on what was important. It's no wonder that so many severance meetings include words or phrases referring to a lack of fit, team sensitivity, and alignment. The new management wisdom highlights getting the right people in the right seats, so it's not surprising that an increasing number of managers even openly admit in exit meetings conditions such as, "You were clearly hired with expectations on which we didn't even have consensus among ourselves," or "You brought in a lot of new ideas and challenged us, but we were not ready for the round peg quite yet." Companies need to consider adding new seats instead of simply placing people in those that already exist.

That said, the likelihood of a visionary's or change agent's ability to have an impact will directly reflect his or her ability to align management around what is important—in essence, to change thinking from how to keep things running smoothly and avoiding disruption to how to start running things effectively to achieve focused and perhaps radical growth. It is the shift from being satisfied with the present to being obsessed with results, from being comfortable to being visionary. Only then will radical ideas be perceived as relevant and important instead of frivolous or, much too commonly, threatening.

A key issue for the DVS employee is timing. Too often, the excitement and the grasp of what could be is its own downfall. People resist change. People are suspicious of radical change. And people fear radical change that is proposed too quickly.

The visionary brain clearly sees opportunity on the fast track. It views beyond process and moves to impact. This, however, is not the best way to get others on your side.

STEPS TO ALIGNMENT

In a typical visionary or idea presentation, progress is taken for granted. In the disposable visionary's mind, change is assumed as not only acceptable but also preferable. New ideas are obviously something to be valued. However, in most organizations, management does not want revolutionary change. It wants new ways to keep things the way they are. Patrick Lencioni highlighted this when he listed the first failing in his *The Five Temptations of a CEO* as a tendency to put preservation of the status quo over a passionate pursuit of results.[3] It is a common issue, and if it is prevalent at the top, most politically sensitive managers will prefer to follow rather than challenge it.

Given the insider resistance to radical change, the disposable visionary will need to understand that most will not share his or her shortcut perception of why a new idea might be worthy of consideration, much less implementation. They will need to be guided. This will be frustrating, but so is moving too fast with the result of moving on or being asked to move out just as quickly.

This is why a visionary must first accept that new ideas need time to gain acceptance. Opportunities may be lost temporarily, but having others aligned will save time in the long run and job searches in the short run.

FLIP YOUR FOCUS

Most visionaries have experienced situations where management defers to the status quo over vision. And the way many visionaries present new ideas only forces management to prove this perception repeatedly. As stated in the first chapter, 48 percent of change agents hired to make a difference found that their company or boss was not open to change, new ideas, or new ways of thinking.

In the typical sequence of discussion, the words preceding a change presentation are, "Do you have a few minutes for me to share an idea that could help our business?" (or increase sales, or enhance customer loyalty, or expand our product line, etc.). This is followed by the idea, the cost, an analysis of what it would take to implement, and finally how the idea fits into the corporate strategic process. The following illustrates this sequence:

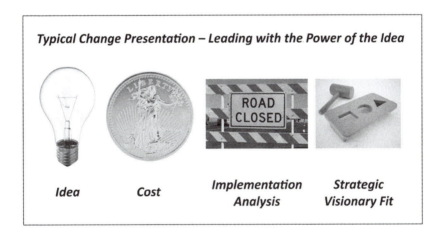

Photo Sources: Edokter, U.S. Mint, Martyhaas/Dreamstime.com, and Hakan Doğu/Dreamstime.com

To those listening, this can be easily and naturally perceived as an idea that will "disrupt operations at a cost we don't need to spend, to create chaos we don't want to endure, with new processes that we don't want to impose."

Forget the impact on vision and growth. Corporate vision will never be adjusted to accept ideas that force change in a way that is seen as more trouble than it's worth.

The safest decision is always to say no, or to say yes in ways that minimize risk.

Using this order of presentation, it is no surprise that new ideas are rejected quickly and absolutely. The expected result will be, essentially "That's too radical a thought . . . that will divert resources needed elsewhere . . . into a process that will disrupt our activity . . . and achieve an outcome we don't need."

The bigger the opportunity, the greater the risk of change. The greater the risk of change, the more resistance you will face. The more resistance you face, the greater is the likelihood that someone will be personally challenged and intimidated. That's why the presentation of a new idea needs to flip this process:

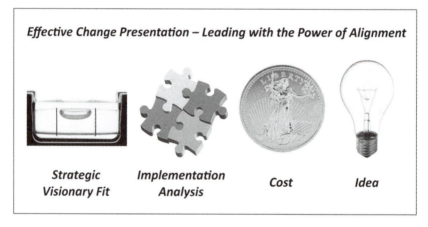

Effective Change Presentation – Leading with the Power of Alignment

Strategic Visionary Fit   **Implementation Analysis**   **Cost**   **Idea**

Photo Sources: Accessony/Dreamstime.com, Amada44, U.S. Mint, and Edokter

Start with the assurance of a strategic fit, then give analysis of how this fits and the issues it addresses, followed by budgetary understanding and its potential impact or ROI, and finally the breakthrough concept. It is an alignment process that ensures that each step is accepted before any new ideas are presented.

STRATEGIC ALIGNMENT IS ESSENTIAL BUT NOT EASY

Establishing the strategic fit requires a clear understanding of what matters to the company in the short term and the long term. It involves a breakdown of what the fulfillment of the mission looks like. It should also break down barriers to anything that prevents the ultimate achievement of the mission.

But alignment around the mission is not easy. In a meeting with eight C-level managers of a pharmaceutical company, one of the authors asked them to describe the company's mission statement. The eight leaders presented five different interpretations of their mission statement. What made these differences even more striking was that, just 60 days previously, they had all attended an intensive weeklong mission strategy session. Within two months, half of them had lost their alignment with the company's vision, their purpose, and the measurements of its success.

Since group resistance is stronger and creates barriers for revisiting issues in the future, alignment should start with individuals. Starting at the top is best, but any influencer can be the key to success. As mentioned earlier, champions make the best partners. It is not important whether you lead the charge or someone else picks up the torch. What is important is that you begin to create agreement on a future vision with key players.

As a side note, network and alliance building is not just meeting with influencers; it also means building their confidence in the vision and continued alignment with what is important and how you plan to help achieve it. A network of influencers needs to be fed with ongoing data and support to reinforce their commitment to an idea. They need to believe that their trust and excitement is based on objective information—not just one person's perspective. Therefore, continue to provide trends, research, white papers, social media activity, and marketplace shifts and behavior that make a vision not just an option but a logical part of the future.

A good place to start is a one-on-one session with an internal champion who shares the goal of moving the company dramatically forward. It could be the president, VP of product development, chief branding officer, CFO, chief of staff, or any person in a position or department of influence. These discussions usually begin with a foundational question such as, "What is the single most important measurement that shows we are achieving our vision to its fullest potential?" Or "How would we measure our ability to become absolutely indispensable to our customers?" Also be sure to discover "What has prevented us from pursuing these types of goals in the past?" This should be a free exchange of ideas and points of view. Resist the urge to drive your specific agenda forward; be open to leadership's concept of what is important to the company and the process to get there. Perhaps the most important guideline is to spend at least as much time actively listening as you do sharing your ideas.

From this meeting, a group session might arise. If this occurs, it needs the same aspirational approach. It should not be seen as a brainstorming session. These are famous for their ability to raise more obstacles than opportunities. Greater success is found when the meeting is given a new name and thus a new objective. If possible, try to establish a dreamstorming session. This creates a meeting environment whose stated purpose is to pursue change. The ground rules are different, and the attendees have a different expectation of the outcome and their roles.

The key combination to success in such a meeting is to merge the traditional with the new. This minimizes the perceived disruption by recognizing the strengths and value of what has gone before or is currently in place. It specifically identifies the following in Table 7.1:

Table 7.1   Combining Tradition and Aspiration

The Traditional— Our Comfort Zone	Combines with	The Aspirational— Our Dreams
1. What currently makes us unique?	►	What enables us to be indispensable?
2. What is the strength of our culture?	►	Is there anything about us that prevents us from becoming a category of one that sets us apart from anyone else?
3. What has been our greatest achievement?	►	What would be the ultimate vision—our dream achievement?
4. How do we know we have been successful?	►	What would be the greatest measurement of our success?
5. What has been the greatest attribute of our people?	►	What has been the most underutilized talent of our people?
6. What has been the greatest freedom our culture provides?	►	What has been the greatest barrier our culture has presented?

By combining these two elements of tradition and aspiration through the resolution of these six issues, we are able to create the "dirty dozen" of alignment. The results will provide the unity, direction, and freedom for innovation that maximizes the vision for innovation while minimizing the perceived disruption and challenge to the status quo.

Once there is agreement and excitement concerning the vision and the outcome, the rest falls into place.

IMPLEMENTATION ANALYSIS: SHIFTING FROM DISRUPTION TO OPPORTUNITY

Like a snowball gaining speed rolling downhill, once a visionary alignment is in place, the change has the power to pick up speed. Those who create obstacles may now be seen as preventers of progress rather than as protectors of the past. In moving toward presentation, the next two stages involve an assurance of acceptance and an understanding of value.

Collective denial is a strong force, along with collective amnesia, so framing the problem and the opportunity in a manner that management can clearly respect and value (such as time, money, sales opportunities, or customers lost) is a necessary step toward acceptance of new ideas, even if they clearly align with the company's strategy. Instead of addressing cost and the barriers of development, the flipped approach identifies the cultural and perceived operational issues. In this phase, consider identifying the following:

1. How have previous change initiatives been championed and implemented?
2. What does this tell us about the ideal process for introducing change or new programs/products?
3. Which departments are critical to acceptance?
4. What were the key reasons past change initiatives and their proponents were deemed inappropriate, and what should we learn from that?
5. What company strengths can we build on that make any innovation both appropriate for our growth and successful in its application?
6. Who are the power players or key decision influencers who have the biggest say, and does this align with their vision for the company as well as their personal aspirations?

The first four questions identify the issues that are critical to implementing new innovation and vision. Question 5 is the stimulus that creates the logical flow that reduces the disruption of the first four issues. It creates the perception that this is the right path toward the future and not a detour from past investments. It builds on the current market equity that the company has created throughout its history.

The last question is the one that seems to derail most change. This is the issue that most often rears its head and results in almost half of change agents feeling that the overall environment is resistant to change. It is usually key power plays and power players that derail visionary change. Overcoming this usually rests in either understanding how to win over these areas or having a champion who can provide a power play of his or her own.

COST: DECIDING WHETHER TO INVEST IN THE PAST OR THE FUTURE

Cost includes money, time, resources (usually people), and overcoming political pride. The latter is a growing currency in stagnant cultures and should not be taken lightly. An effective illustrative formula for the implementation of innovative change is as follows:

$$\text{Value} = \frac{\text{Indispensability Impact } (C \times F \times E \times B)^* \times \text{Accepted Alignment}}{(\text{Time} \times \$ \times \text{People}) \text{ Pride Factor}}$$

* Cheaper × Faster × Easier × Better

The opportunity to create value—and your chances for acceptance as a change agent—is a reflection of how well you can communicate that your ideas deliver a level of impact against the resources necessary to deliver it.

In this formula, value is perceived as a result of

1. Perceived impact to deliver the next generation of what is important. In its highest level, it is the pursuit of something that is preemptively indispensable to your customers, shareholders, membership, or audience. This will be evaluated on the basis of being Cheaper (C), Faster (F), Easier (E), or Better (B). The more it achieves or delivers one or more of these benefits, the great its impact. "Better" is often highly subjective, and the more objective it can become through customer research, competitive growth, or market trends, the stronger the case for it.
2. These elements of impact are evaluated against the time, dollars, and human resources necessary to deliver it. The lower the demand on these resources, the greater the value. The greater the demand on these resources, the higher the impact will need to be.
3. The cost can also be directly increased by obstacles caused by the personal pride of those who do not agree with this idea, the idea of change in general, or the fact that people were not part of the initial discussion.
4. All factors are amplified by how well everything is aligned with the visionary aspiration of the organization. The higher the alignment with and the excitement about goals within that vision, the greater the internal value.

In leveraging this formula, it's clear that the more time can be reduced, the greater the value will be. This is why it is important to sometimes present work as "in progress." This shortens the perceived delivery time, since value or excitement has been delivered quickly with interim success. It shows that progress has already been made through the resources already invested and that continued and perhaps increased investment is justified.

This also continues to reinforce and confirm the fit with the strategic vision through intermittent approvals and thus ensures ongoing alignment on the progress and the potential value. Finally, this helps to offset the issues of pride, as it allows time for acceptance, input, and personal investment from senior management. They are part of the process.

Surprises, even pleasant ones, are seldom welcomed. They remind others that they were not in the loop. This implies that the opinions of others are not valued. It can corner people into quick judgments. None of these are helpful in the presentation or execution of a new idea.

As an example, visionary director Steven Spielberg almost lost the chance to finish the movie *Close Encounters of the Third Kind*. While the studio originally liked the concept, their limited visionary alignment also had a cost limitation. In addition, the director continuously watched other movies every night during the production, giving him new ideas and budget increases to include throughout the filming. When the studio saw the potential budget and time overruns and saw that they had not been informed of the need or opportunities for ongoing changes—even those Spielberg thought were essential for the vision of the film—they contacted the director and essentially fired him. In this situation, distance and current investment allowed the director to ignore the message. He completed the film, which went on to gross over $288 million ($116.39 million in North America and $171.7 million in foreign countries) on a total budget of $19.4 million.[4] It became, but almost didn't become, Columbia Pictures's most successful film at that time.

Using steps of information, achievement reports, and impact updates that fit into the value equation, even change resisters are engaged in the change process and become part of its commitment. The result is a perception that change is needed progress, not an avoidable problem. The challenge is to integrate the analysis of how visionary innovation will create something that is faster, easier, better, or cheaper while developing it within an agreed and engaged use of time, cost, and resources with a process that addresses personal pride, participation, and an understanding of necessary change.

THE IDEA: NOT AN INSPIRATION BUT AN IMPACT

Through this process, the final presentation of innovative change is not seen as an intrusion but instead as a necessary improvement. It is not one person's idea but instead the collaboration of an organization's key influencers to support progress. It is a joint passion to bring an idea to life without the fear of uprooting an entire company, although that may often be the greatest need.

To make the final step even more effective, it should involve both the presentation itself and the ones presenting. If at all possible, leverage internal allies with the greatest political clout to lead the charge and set up the concepts. This is why finding internal mentors and supporters is a key to success. It also reflects the fact that the most successful leaders spend a lot of their time networking internally and externally. It builds alliances and incorporates the experience, counsel, and vital success of others. It is vital that the strategic purpose and the impact of the vision are clearly stated. Ideas do not stand on their own merit; they stand on their power to change the playing field.

The ideas that have the greatest impact will have the greatest internal challenges. Therefore, they need the greatest positioning of their impact.

The Smothers Brothers did not simply offer a new variety show. They provided a voice for a new generation that would change the direction of television audiences. The adult audience was being replaced by 18- to 24-year-olds seeking a new young-adult outlet on television. This revolutionized the direction of television as well as creating a more entertaining and edgy program.

The first Chrysler minivan, often recognized as saving the Chrysler Corporation in the1980s, was rejected for years. It was regarded as a misfit in how cars were being designed. Since it served a family, it was rejected by the chief engineer of the Dodge Truck division: "It's not a truck."[5] The management "experts" also felt that following was always safer than leading: "Ford and GM don't have one, so there must not be a demand." However, after being shelved for years, the minivan still had a few champions who would not let the idea die. New CEO Lee Iacocca eventually reexamined the design and saw its potential as a "suburban family mover." The bean counters initially tried to block it as well, stating that they didn't have the funds for it. But the key champions stayed the course. Research confirmed the vehicle's potential. The champions continued to push for its production; finding ways to leverage existing car chassis for production efficiency, they changed the future of both Chrysler and the auto industry.

In another example seen in the John Lasseter profile at the end of this chapter, computer animation failed to reach acceptance when presented as an efficient way to provide background art, but it changed the industry when it was perceived as the way to create an entirely new experience in storytelling. Thus it was not a replacement for traditional animation; it opened up the challenge to stretch moviemaking through a new technology.

Sometimes it is not the idea itself but the vision for what the idea stands for that makes it acceptable and exciting. Beyond the impact of ROI, support by key influencers will establish a foundation for the vision of change. How it fits with the corporate strategy and with the current management, leadership, and labor creates the passion and commitment to see it through to its fullest potential.

So what does this mean?

No one is an island, and few ideas will stand on their own. Visionary employees bring a passion and a broader vision that few will immediately grasp. While the visionary may be able to leap to how an impact might be made, others will need to walk first and see it in steps. Others need to contribute along the way and, ideally, perceive that they are leading the cause. An understanding of how something brings value and how the cost of change can be minimized is critical for the acceptance by others and their potential to help champion a cause. Don't present ideas that others have to chase. Share ideas that others can embrace, accept, and own. After all, it is better to promote a good idea than to promote your exit.

JOHN LASSETER

WHY SHOULD DISNEY LISTEN TO AN EMPLOYEE VISIONARY, WHEN THEY CAN BUY HIM BACK LATER FOR ONLY $7.4 BILLION?

In the 1980s two animation visionaries worked for the Walt Disney Corporation: Tim Burton and John Lasseter. In addition to their employment by Disney as budding animation artists, they share another common bond. They were both fired by Disney, and for the same reasons: challenging the status quo in animation and storylines. Interestingly, they would both share the honor of being reunited with Disney years later.

Burton went on to become one of the most influential directors in Hollywood—the inspiring leader behind such films as *Beetlejuice*, the Michael Keaton *Batman* movies, *The Nightmare Before Christmas*, *Edward Scissorhands*, and *The Planet of the Apes* reboot. But before that, he worked for Disney where he created and presented an animated short film called *Frankenweenie*, about a boy who brings his dead dog back to life. Unfortunately, Burton did not screen this with his supervisor. Deemed too dark for Disney, Burton was fired. Ironically, while Burton was later creating a name for himself as one of the most innovative and creative directors, he entered into a partnership with Disney. His first project was a full-length stop-motion animated version of *Frankenweenie*, which was released by Disney Studios in 2012. Completing the irony, the main character, Sparky, has a tombstone in the pet cemetery outside of Haunted Mansion Holiday, a seasonal attraction at Disneyland.

The cost of letting John Lasseter go ran a bit higher. Lasseter is responsible for . . . well, let's just say he's one of the brains behind Pixar.

(*Continued*)

While at Disney, Lasseter and producer Thomas L. Wilhite pitched an idea to create *The Brave Little Toaster* using traditionally animated characters inside the then expensive computer-generated backgrounds. On a perceived cost basis, the animation administrator and Disney's president at the time rejected the presentation. Apparently, they also went around their bosses to present the idea without their approval. Within minutes of the meeting, Lasseter was fired.

Sometime earlier, Lasseter had met Ed Catmull, vice president at the computer graphics division for George Lucas's Industrial Light and Magic (ILM). Catmull recognized the passion and vision of Lasseter and hired him as the first animator at ILM in 1983. With a new set of colleagues, Lasseter produced a short film that used computerized characters as well as the background for the first time.

In 1986 Steve Jobs bought ILM's digital division for $10 million and founded Pixar. Jobs continued to invest in the studio—and in Catmull and Lasseter—for ten years before it became profitable. During that time, Pixar was producing animated commercials and shorts. Then came Pixar's first computer animated feature—something called *Toy Story*.

Fast forward to 2006. During this time, Pixar and Lasseter revolutionized movie animation with films such as *A Bug's Life*, *Toy Story 2*, *Monsters, Inc.*, *Finding Nemo*, *The Incredibles*, and *Cars*. Some were released as joint efforts with Disney. In April 2006, Disney recognized the need to bring in the capabilities, technology, and visionary personnel that Pixar had developed.

Disney purchased Pixar for $7.4 billion and put Catmull and Lasseter in charge of invigorating the Walt Disney Animation Studios. Lasseter became chief creative officer of both Pixar and Walt Disney Animation Studios and principal creative adviser at Walt Disney Imagineering. He now reports directly to Disney chief Bob Iger, bypassing Disney's studio executives.

This decision—and the permission for Pixar to retain the culture, vision, and quality it had established—helped to catapult the animation revival at Disney with films including *Cars 2*, *Up*, *Brave*, *Tangled*, and the most profitable animated film of all time, *Frozen*, with $1.072 billion worldwide, which passed Pixar/Disney's *Toy Story 3* at number two.

Unlike those who dismissed him, Lasseter recognizes the need to empower people and allow evolution—even revolution—within a company. One of his associates admires the way he's "making Disney a filmmaker-driven studio" versus an executive-driven one and how he's "allowed the Disney culture to continue to evolve."[6,7]

Chapter 8

How to Manage Yourself as a DVS Employee

You can't change a company from the unemployment line

Let him that would move the world first move himself.

Socrates

Is DVS always terminal? Sadly, under most conditions, it seems to be . . . unless properly managed. Your vision as a DVS employee often can exceed the ability of the organization or its management to leverage your potential. However, properly managed, the relationship between an organization and its DVS employees, and the opportunities it brings, can prosper and result in tremendous growth. As outlined in Chapter 7 and later chapters, when management changes or adjusts its attitudes and priorities toward DVS employees, there can be a dramatic impact on the entire organization. And the most effective change happens when management leverages your DVS potential, setting high standards for you and others to follow.

However, even if management changes do occur, your DVS tendencies may still be perceived as threatening and inappropriate. Therefore, you should still adjust your own style to increase your perceived value and to preserve—or at least extend—your employment while still striving for breakthrough change and innovation. After all, you can't change anything from outside the organization. You're also not going to change the direction of the boat by treading water, whether you're inside the organization or outside. So, the key is not just to keep your job—you've seen too many who make that their primary goal—but to keep it in a way that still gives you the opportunity to make a difference within the organization.

The necessary or appropriate steps may vary depending on the type of organization you work for. Some of these will be discussed later in Chapter 8. But here are 13 guidelines that will enhance your ability to contribute to any organization. Because you're a visionary, you'll probably want to take each of these points to a new level in ways that the authors have not yet envisioned. That's the fun part about having DVS: you're always looking for ways to improve things.

THIRTEEN GUIDELINES FOR EFFECTIVE DVS GROWTH AND IMPACT

1. Show Value

Focus on what is really important, and quantify your expectations. Remember, there are really only two ways to evaluate any innovation or change: how it increases revenue and how it reduces cost. Even traditional soft issues, such as customer satisfaction, loyalty, employee motivation, customer service, production renovation, PR, or advertising breakthroughs must be measurable and relate to the bottom line. If the change you propose is truly meaningful to the customer, it will reward the company financially, but you must show this bottom-line impact in your thinking. By carefully building a strong case for your innovations, you'll be able to challenge your own logic for changes before someone else does, and you'll be able to reinforce it. Almost every new idea requires a leap of faith, but by working out the details, you can make the leap as short as possible for the decision makers who consider it.

CLAIRE'S STORY

Claire was a product manager for a pharmaceutical firm. She had an idea to enhance sales by distributing free software preloaded with prescription information. The company was obsessed with ROI (return on investment) that depended on the number of prescriptions written, but real-time prescription numbers were impossible to obtain. Rather than chucking the concept, Claire introduced a "return on idea" process that established measurements for other indirect factors that drove sales. These included (1) increased time that sales reps were able to spend with doctors, (2) follow-up surveys that measured doctors' positive perceptions of the company, (3) top-of-mind recall of their product over the competition's, and (4) doctors' ability to state the product's benefits. Her new process resulted in a successful program launch, established a precedent for measuring other new programs, and gained Claire the internal respect she so richly deserved. Not bad for a disposable visionary!

2. Have the Audacity to Become Indispensable to Your Customers

But as you become indispensable, be sure you understand what is most important to them in becoming a partner in their success. Nothing will drive change more effectively than presenting ideas from your customers' viewpoint. It is not enough to offer a "good" product or service. It is not enough to have "satisfied" customers. Unless you are perceived as uniquely qualified to become an indispensable partner, you will always be subject to cheaper, faster, or more efficient competition.

Your ideas will always be seen as more palpable if you start with "our customers' primary need is . . .", "our customers have chosen us over our competitors because . . . ", or "our customers' biggest challenge or problem is . . ." and then end it with a visionary concept that will preempt the playing field.

In 2000, a major professional association measured the satisfaction levels of its members. A DVS employee discovered that current members had the same satisfaction levels as former members! This revelation meant that none of their satisfaction measurements had anything to do with determining whether a member renewed or dropped membership. This discovery changed the playing field. They began to measure whether their members felt that the association and its benefits were indispensable to their professional and personal success, which revealed the critical areas the organization needed to focus on.

Radical change was accepted, and the association reorganized around member segments based on what programs would meet the criterion of being indispensable. They enjoyed a double-digit increase in membership growth for the first time in decades.

3. Carefully Filter Your Own Ideas, Through Yourself and Through Others

When you speak, talk about things that have a positive impact, not about your own frustrations. Otherwise, your desire to improve the organization may be misinterpreted as negativism. Don't try to change too much or too often. Remember that most people and organizations don't deal well with change and deal even worse with a lot of change. So be your own best filter. Make sure that you are perceived as someone who talks about change only when it can create a tangible difference. Offer concepts, not complaints. Concentrate on the big things that matter for the organization in what you do, what you talk about, and what becomes your passion. Sometimes a little thing can have a big impact. If so, then it's not a little thing.

The following series of "Do I know?" questions is not a bad way for DVS employees to start each Monday morning. If you can't answer these questions, then you may be pursuing your own agenda and could find yourself in deep Pursuit of Other Opportunities:

- Do I know what is most important to my boss? Alternatively, do I know what places the greatest pressure on my boss?
- Do I know the two most important issues affecting the short-term performance of this company?
- Do I know the two most important issues affecting the long-term performance of this company?
- Do I know the greatest competitive risk to this company?
- Do I know how anything I propose will impact any of the above issues?

Focus your attention and your discussions on things that matter. If you can't answer these questions, find the answers. Better yet, if the answers aren't readily available, find ways to help identify them for the company!

4. Become an Obsessive Listener and a Selective Conversationalist

Even when you know the answer, consider asking questions first. This serves three very important purposes. First, you'll hear others' perceptions and objections. This will help you learn about potential support or obstacles before you present your own thoughts. Second, you'll show that you are more interested in using the input of others than in promoting yourself. As you know from previous chapters, DVS employees are seldom out to promote themselves, but they are often misunderstood by those who are intimidated by change. Third, you'll knock down walls by creating a more open environment for others to own part of the change you want to implement.

It's not just important to listen. It is just as important to be perceived as objective or nonjudgmental in your responses. Give others the chance to look good. Your questions can help guide them or enhance their own ideas. Set the standard for encouragement and support of others. The rewards will be tremendous as you begin understanding other points of view and gain a reputation as a good listener. Consider the following techniques in your next business meeting or one-on-one discussion.

Understand your body language. DVS employees tend to telegraph disapproval and impatience by crossing their arms, tapping a pencil, or sighing loudly in meetings. Sit up or lean forward slightly to show attentiveness. Because they get bored with the mundane or start thinking about what really matters to them, DVS employees are apt to drift or doze in meetings (you know you do), so focus on the implications. *Do* play a mental search game: try to find something of value in what is being said, and take notes. In particular, carefully observe what the senior people respond to. This presents the right message, and you'll have information to leverage in presenting your own ideas. *Don't* resort to the old trick of wearing a rubber band around your wrist and snapping it whenever you get bored or start to nod off. You may tell your coworkers that you're doing it to quit a bad habit (you fill in the blank—smoking, eating, coffee, sex, etc.), but you could end up with permanent scars, especially after budget meetings.

The eyes have it—be careful how you use them. Maintain eye contact to the degree that you and the person you are listening to are comfortable. Be careful of the "DVS eye-roll," an involuntary response that occurs when confronted with a truly dumb or politically driven idea. The eye-roll is almost as difficult to stop as a sneeze, so if you feel one coming on, *do* politely interrupt and draw a visual summary or outline of the points being made. Everyone likes a chart. This not only shows understanding but also helps the other person reevaluate his own points. It also gives you a break from staring at an empty suit. *Don't* rely on eye drops to mask your eye-rolling. If the dumb ideas are flying thick and fast, you'll look like you're crying as much on the outside as you are on the inside.

Respond appropriately. Look for opportunities to move the thoughts of others down your path. Respond objectively but also with a purpose. This a rare approach in business, and others will find it intriguing. *Do* offer leading statements or comments such as, "So if I follow your logic, we can assume the customer will . . ." or "That certainly provides production with some interesting efficiency opportunities, doesn't it?" *Don't* keep saying, "Tell me more about that" and "What do you think we should do?" If all this sounds familiar, it should. Your psychiatrist has been using the same techniques on you for years. But your goal is to gain more information about potential concerns, not to fill in the hour.

Make your point, and shut up. When you find the right opportunity, strike while the iron is hot. *Do* build on the points that support your vision, but don't try to win the war all by yourself. Ask for input: "If we based a new sales plan on this information, what would it include?" Nudge the direction. *Don't* force the issue or ask yes-or-no questions that could shut down the concept. For you to make the point and then let others make the decision is a powerful combination. Avoid pushing acceptance or the timetable with questions like, "Isn't this a great idea?" or "Aren't we ready to make a decision?" You're selling a new concept, not a used car.

5. Get Clarity While You Are Listening

Effective listening also helps you clarify the other person's point of view on important issues. This is especially important with your boss and other key influencers. While you don't want to keep asking the obvious ("Can you tell me what our mission statement means again?"), you should strive for clarity that prepares you to react quickly when you see new opportunities. Use reviews and MBO sessions to confirm how your work is aligned with the corporate vision. Get agreement on your objectives and the bigger picture. You are seeking guidelines and implied, or better yet, established permission. Remember, when seeking clarity, ask pointed questions and keep yourself in an open frame of mind.

Incorporate the following steps into regular meetings with your boss, and if he doesn't have regular meetings with you, request them.

Focus solely on what the other person is saying.

DO try hard to understand his or her point of view, instead of thinking about how to refute it.

DON'T use sarcasm, and above all else, resist the overwhelming temptation to interrupt with "Right," "Sure," or "Of course" when you hear the obvious. These make the same impression as saying "Duh!" at the point when your boss is telling you what he feels you need to hear. This will shut down the conversation and, if you're talking with your boss, will quickly precipitate your Pursuit of Other Opportunities.

Keep an open mind.

DO wait until the other person is finished before deciding that you disagree. If you find yourself considering the source, then you're engaging in the same judgmental behavior that others apply to you as a disposable visionary.

DON'T make assumptions about what the other person is thinking. Even though the other person may not be a visionary, he or she may actually have the kernel of a new idea or may give you constructive criticism that will help you promote your own idea. Everyone has the potential to be a visionary, as demonstrated by the sudden outbreak of new ideas that happens each year when budget time rolls around.

When getting direction from someone who challenges your ideas, wait until they finish to get all the information you can to defend your thinking.

DON'T jump in to defend yourself too soon.

DO respond only after you have all the information. Make sure you ask, "Is there anything else?" before you even think of responding.

DON'T use the desperate ploy of placing copious amount of coffee, water, and salted nuts in front of them to get them out of the room. Most politically astute reactionary (PAR) employees have a much larger bladder capacity than DVS employees, due to their uncanny ability to sit through long and pointless meetings. Besides, it's important to hear all the negatives. Let them "wax on" so you'll know how to "wax off."

As you work to develop listening skills, you may feel a bit unnerved if there is a natural pause in the conversation. What should you say next? Remember that it's not always up to you to fill in dead space. Learn to settle into the silence, take a backseat temporarily, and use it get a better view of where the boat is going.

6. Avoid Anything That Could Get You Labeled as a "Loose Cannon"

There are many labels that DVS employees bear with pride: "maverick," "pioneer," "renegade," "visionary," "change agent," even "instigator." They all reflect movement and action. They also can be very misunderstood and resented. If someone asks you to describe yourself, look at descriptions that add value: "revenue enhancer," "business developer," "customer service advocate," or "performance motivator." Of all the labels that stir up negative impressions about team playing and cooperation, "loose cannon" is the most damaging. And while you may not call yourself that, as a disposable visionary, you are often given that label. It suggests that your initiatives aren't aligned with the priorities of the organization, and it carries an impression that you might be pursuing your own agenda.

A loose cannon is usually associated with poor focus, not poor ideas. Remember Barbara in Chapter 1, who introduced action figures and home equity credit lines? She could have avoided her "loose cannon" label simply by going to the company's real, not stated, power structures and probing their needs. Based on their concerns that "we need to expand into the young male market" and "we can't target when people specifically need money," she could have built an image of working within the company and solving problems that are vexing others. Instead of being perceived as "Ready, Fire, Aim" she could have presented her case in a more logical manner and established herself as being distinctive rather than disruptive.

To avoid this label, watch your attitude and ensure that your activities are aligned with the way the organization measures success.

7. Make Your Boss Wildly Successful

Unless you run your own business, you are accountable to someone else. Just as you seek to build up others, don't forget that your boss is one of the most important "others" that you work with. DVS employees have a tendency to view their boss as an obstacle to dramatic change and the keeper of the political scepter. Often, this is true. However, he or she is also charged with enhancing company performance. If your boss reads this book, especially Chapter 10, "How to Manage the DVS Employee," you could have an immediate ally. But even if he or she doesn't, you can at least prevent your boss from becoming the source of your termination.

You can help your boss to be the boss she wants to be. Think of her as a project for you; just as you see areas for corporate improvement, you should see your boss as a potential superstar that could use your help. The key is to keep her informed on work-in-process in a way that uses her talents. Seek her input, and look for opportunities to make her look good. Just as you would give peers or your staff credit for team efforts, find ways to leverage your boss and enable her to be a leader in your initiatives.

Long-tenured DVS employees, a rare but successful breed, usually bite one of the hardest bullets: they meet regularly with their boss. They also take a page from sports teams: all successful team meetings need to have an agenda and end with the ability for all participants to immediately perform better. In meeting with your boss, use this time to (1) get agreement on the most pressing issue(s) to the company and your boss, (2) communicate what you are doing to help, (3) discuss any changes that you have taken since your last meeting that your boss needs to know—remember that surprises are seldom appreciated, even pleasant ones—and (4) identify issues that need to be resolved that prevent your or your boss's success. Most crucial, however, is for your boss to understand that you are there to support him or her. The meetings should always end with, "Is there anything else coming down on you or your boss that I can help resolve or should integrate into what I'm doing?" You'll not only get direction but also an ally and regularly scheduled free lunches if you plan it right.

8. Give People—Especially Your Boss—What They Ask For

But also look for the right opportunity to enhance or change things. Sometimes this means combining what they say they want with what they really need. Sometimes it means asking for their input and mentioning your ideas in the process. Sometimes it means waiting for another time. Remember, most people, especially non-DVS employees, don't like constant change. They get tired of the continuous new ideas, even if they are exactly what need to be done. Be patient, and watch the level of arguments. If you are presenting conflicting or radically different approaches to the conventional wisdom, ask yourself the following questions, and be prepared to detail the answers:

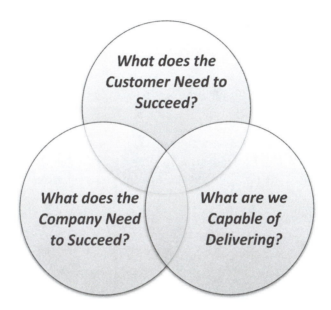

Finding ways to confirm that you are within the vision of what is important to the individual, the organization, and the customer is a powerful threefold criterion for any recommendation. These questions can verify that what is being asked for really fits, and they can underscore the value of your input. Once you have the answers to these questions, gradually you can begin to raise the issues and potential alternatives. Many DVS employees force issues in an "either we do it your way or my way" ultimatum. Present your alternatives as strong, integrated opportunities, not strong resistance to what others want.

Beware the Boss's Pets. In providing your boss with what he or she wants, be aware that there will be conditions that will impact whether an idea is truly acceptable or not. The biggest obstacles will be processes, perceptions, and people.

Pet Processes: Every boss has instituted some key procedures that they felt were vital to the organization. Find out these are, and be very careful not to change them too quickly. Everything from customer service to email policies may need radical overhauling, but if they are your boss's pet priorities, think of addressing the underlying processes later.

One boss actually determined that 24-hour turnaround of all email was critical to the organization—no matter how trivial the messages were or how much they promoted a culture of passing the buck. Change agents failed to have any impact until they recognized the sacred role that processes played in their boss's criteria of success—even when they were a major part of the problem in productivity, teamwork, and accountability.

Pet Perceptions: Bosses will have their own perceptions of reality. This will include what is broken and what are the measurements of success. Be sure you have an accurate understanding of those perceptions before you try to change them or, more importantly, before you try to challenge what your boss has been telling the next level of management is acceptable.

Pet Personnel: Every boss has some preferred staff members whom they believe are invaluable. Know who these people are, and handle them with care. They may even be deadwood on your own staff, but they reflect your boss's judgment. By pointing out their faults, you are indirectly criticizing your boss's ability to evaluate character. This is very risky and usually leads to DVS fulfillment very quickly.

"You can take that off now, honey, you're home."

"Take what off?"

In this case you, have three options: (1) ignore their poor performance or PAR tendencies; (2) try to incorporate them into your vision and get their support, although you will usually find they are better at leveraging their preferred status and waiting you out; or (3) carefully document their resistance in an objective way while you gather support from other champions to back your initiatives. As with the other two pet areas, don't ever feel the need to move quickly to address personnel issues when there is an emotional tie. PAR employees share a common bond that can be dangerous to break, especially when it's between your boss and someone confronting your success.

9. Respect and Leverage Office Politics

Sorry, this is sacrilege to someone with DVS. It's like asking a dog not to scratch fleas. Politics can be an irritant, and we would all like to live without them. They are a very real problem in almost every organization, but you don't need to change your own passion. Don't lower your standards. Don't change your ethics. Don't lose your focus on the big picture. And don't lose your dreams or your insight into where the company can be going. However, do pay attention to the expected courtesies and traditions of the organization, and where possible, look to use them to your advantage. Understand the value of small talk, even if it seems as pointless as a Chicago weather forecast. Get to know the personal sides of others, including your boss. Once you understand what is important to him or her, leverage it in your initiatives by tying the objective into what is personally important to your boss, or boss's boss, or even other departments, in order to create the internal support necessary for final implementation.

You might consider looking at company politics as if they were a business challenge: you have to use them, it's time-intensive if you want to change them, and if you don't use them, someone else will. So take it as a challenge. Examine how you can incorporate politics into what you feel is the most important outcome for the organization. Very often, politics will help you to create the team that you need to effectively implement changes. You need technical, procedural, operational, and sales people as well as political operatives to make an idea work. Identify the real power brokers in the organization, and bring them into the program. Associating with points of power increases the acceptance and likelihood of a final implementation as well as your own credibility.

10. Don't One-Up Others on the Spot

Instead, be patient, and don't push to get in the last word. One very consistent trait of DVS employees is that they don't know when to shut up. This is particularly true when the purpose of a discussion or meeting is to evaluate your specific recommendations. As a DVS employee, you are naturally passionate about your ideas and their potential. You get frustrated when others don't get it. And on behalf of your customers and even your company, you want others to see the same vision you do. A very common complaint by senior executives of DVS employees is "They don't know when to quit." This does not mean that you should let ideas die. But there is a time and a place to push.

There are three important times to remember this guideline:

First, when others present their ideas, it is typical for DVS employees to jump in and embellish the idea or take it down a completely different path. Most of the time, the disposable visionary's idea is a better way to go. However, it is often perceived as rude or one-upmanship when one jumps in too quickly. If you must add ideas, do so in a way that gives credit to others. Point out that you are building on another's concept, and ask questions that enable the originator to build on his or her own idea. Be an enabler rather than a controller.

Second, DVS employees often find themselves in heated discussions with others and many times with their boss or senior management. They make the mistake of pushing to get in the last word. While it is natural to defend and promote your vision, it must be done with courtesy and strategic thought. Do so with passion and with substance. When objections are raised, address them with facts, logic, and quantitative support when possible, not with emotion.

When you sense the discussion ending and the idea seems destined for defeat, head it off by asking, "If I can address your concerns in a later meeting, can we have a second forum on this issue?" Get permission, and then sit down. You have won the right to fight again. The biggest mistake DVS employees make is continuing to raise the same points when the meeting is essentially over. It is *never* successful to ask, "Can I just say one more thing?" when the senior member has ended the discussion. Let the senior member have the last word. Let the idea live to be presented another day. The more you push to win on the spot, the less likely it is that you will win anything except a pink slip and the right to engage in the Pursuit of Other Opportunities.

Third, in business politics, it is sometimes better to be perceived as objective than as right. This may seem like a paradox, but arguing too persistently for your idea will convince the people around you that you've lost objectivity, and your personal credibility will suffer. To deal with this situation, you need to be able to convincingly argue the other points of view on your idea.

BEWARE THE GROUP

Group meetings require special care and strategies. PAR employees and conservative managers find safety in numbers. In a meeting, no one has to take personal responsibility for killing an idea. There is truth to a variation on an old adage: "Mediocrity loves company." This is why even informal meetings are in danger of falling into committee environments that can kill or table an idea, or change it beyond recognition.

But meetings are a necessary part of all organizations. Like anything else, they can be a useful blessing or an obstructive curse, depending on whether they grasp the vision or hold to the past. Meetings can be refreshing views into what could be, or they can rehash what has always been done. They happen, and even with champions and preliminary support, the disposable visionary will find himself or herself the lone proponent of what may be seen as uncomfortable change.

But there is hope. When faced with a challenging committee or open discussion, consider using the following proven maneuvers to your advantage:

Enjoy the Circular Discussion. In the early stages of presenting an idea, suggest alternative and opposing viewpoints, and then sit back to see how the discussion develops. Be alert! You may find that someone in the group will support some aspects of your idea that you can build into a sense of co-ownership. Don't let pride of authorship get in your way. Most group discussions are circular in nature, like the Wheel of Fortune. Let the group begin to argue around the positives and negatives. If the idea is truly compelling, the group will usually argue itself back to your original position. At that point, you assume the role of an objective arbiter and say, "What I seem to be hearing is that some issues require further exploration [give a list of those issues], but that the group would like to continue to explore this idea. How should we proceed?" You've just stopped the wheel on the jackpot or at least a free spin. Now you are in a position to take the next steps and assume ownership again.

Delay the Herd Reflex. If the discussion is going against your idea, you may be suffering from something called the "herd reflex." In the herd reflex, a particularly loud, obnoxious, and negative person may be taking control of the discussion, and others in the group follow or are silent for fear of ridicule. Because of this phenomenon, the authors once observed a focus group unanimously conclude that voice messaging would never get off the ground.

If the herd reflex starts happening, try to identify it early. Make sure you have clarified the herd leader's objections, and then cut the meeting short by saying, "You know, these objections deserve more concrete answers than we may have today. I'd like to suggest that we meet again in a week, after we've researched this area." In so doing, you will maintain the aura of objectivity while preventing the early demise of a good idea. You can try waiting out the herd leader by scheduling the next meeting when the person is ill, on vacation, or hopefully Pursuing Other Opportunities. But if this person has real influence, you'll need to deal with his issues eventually. Meet with him, clarify his objections, get him to commit to whatever yardstick (real or imagined) he is using to measure success, and try the meeting again.

Offset with the Negative Sell. If all else fails and the opinion leaders of the meeting start picking apart your idea like piranha on a Big Mac, you can try a somewhat risky maneuver called "the negative sell." This approach best fits when you see that a negative chain reaction is building and rationality has left the building. Interestingly, you can actually take the high road by actually agreeing with the naysayers, "You know, you may be right. This might not work here. We might not be able to handle the change. This could be far too radical and too unique in the marketplace." If the opinion leaders are sufficiently argumentative, they will respond with, "What do you mean we can't handle it? Just because our competition isn't doing it doesn't mean we shouldn't." You could counter with. "Look at the obstacles. We obviously aren't ready to consider this now." Instantly the opinion leaders will become truly indignant and begin thinking about ways to refute your misgivings.

Whether or not they realize what you're doing, you've just created potential advocates for your idea. You've also reinforced your image as objective, because you were willing to step off your high horse. Watch out, though. There are two risks in this approach. One is that the opinion leaders will simply say, "Okay, if you agree we shouldn't do this, we won't. End of discussion."

Usually, though, human ego and contrariness will prevail, and your idea will move on to a new stage of acceptance. It is now perceived as a challenge instead of as an annoyance. The second risk is that by taking their side, you may come off as sarcastic or cynical. This can be avoided if your points are not too personal, such as, "Yes, Fred, your department may not ready for this." You could find out too late that Fred is a black belt, and not in Six Sigma!

Implement the Customer Ownership vs. Competitive Complacency Challenge. This is the most dramatic—and DVS reflective—approach. It brings issues back to their highest level and forces a decision and admission of the organization's objective. It should be used when it appears that a program with obvious customer demand is about to be tabled, or that, once again, the organization is about to turn its back on taking the next step to becoming more competitive. It should also be presented with previous individual discussions to gather some additional internal support.

The presentation goes something like this: "We've had these discussions before, and it seems we have two possible paths, both of which could be appropriate for our company. The first is to continue where we are and maintain our [flat or steady] growth. The other is to consider a radical but still strategically based option that would help us to own the market [or regain substantial share we've lost, or create a buzz in the marketplace that will establish us as the thought leader]."

Most likely, as with the negative sell, this will stimulate some defensiveness and will also lessen the opposition. At this point, be very careful not to push. This strategy is designed to instill new thinking and gain some consideration, not to drive home your point or win the argument.

This strategy will establish your position as an advocate for your company's growth and customer loyalty. It will also help the organization to decide on if and when it wants to break away from "the way we've always done it" and put some action behind its mission and vision statements. However, it should be used primarily with breakthrough concepts that require greater attention but have more potential reward. The best outcome will be to achieve acceptance for the idea in principle and to enable you to further develop it with a task force for a follow-up presentation.

11. Find a Champion

If your boss has limited vision, is too tied to the political game, or provides consistent obstacles to change, you'll need to find someone else internally to support your passion and help present your initiatives. This person may be different from a mentor who guides your career. This is an action-motivated leader who isn't afraid to ruffle the feathers of the organization, who isn't bound by tradition or the status quo, and who has political pull and—if there is such a thing—the magic cloak of security, such as tenure, a dramatic success in the past, or a close relationship with or damaging information about the president. He or she will probably also have DVS tendencies but may have some other indispensable talent that has helped him or her ward off the political hyenas before. Above all else, this person has the respect of the organization.

Use this person for counsel and guidance in developing and presenting breakthrough concepts, as well as someone who might be a future boss. As he or she gets to know your value, they should see your potential power as a member of their team.

12. Form Empowering and Supportive Alliances with Others Who Have the Right Perspective for Change

While a champion provides individual support and essential coaching, the best foundation for your contributions will come from a broad base. Each department may have a few individuals who push the envelope. These are the "yes" thinkers in the "no" departments. Legal, operations, human resources, and branch operations are famous for having hard-liners. Many legal departments have been labeled the "sales-prevention" department, reflecting the long-held belief that no lawyer was ever fired for saying no. However, there will be those in the "no" departments who hold less rigid stances. These are the ones who are essential for paving the way and preparing ideas before they are presented. Their feedback, counsel, and support will allow the DVS employee to locate the real issues that need to be addressed for an idea to be taken seriously.

STEWART'S STORY

A large regional bank used outside legal counsel to review advertising, product ideas, and regulatory compliance. To keep their retainer coming, all the law firm had to do was to keep their client out of trouble and periodically review a contract or two. They understood that the most effective way to protect their client was to be as conservative as possible and find ways to point out the legal reasons to kill or delay controversial initiatives. Most of the attorneys observed this rule religiously.

There was one attorney, Stewart, who would actually listen to ideas and research them thoroughly before making a pronouncement. He looked for the loopholes as well as the obstacles. He became known, somewhat derisively, as the "yes" attorney because he tried to find new ways to make things work within the limitations of laws and regulations. Stewart was a valuable ally because he knew his stuff, and the projects he worked on were uniformly successful. His willingness to seriously consider new ideas and to be a constructive person had a personal toll, however, because Stewart never made partner. You see, Stewart was a fellow DVS sufferer and proud of it.

13. Watch for the Signs of Trouble, from Others and within Yourself

Sometimes, no matter what you do, the disposable visionary in you may not fit with the organization, your boss, or someone with more power than his or her limited visionary ability should be allowed to have. You'll notice certain telltale indications that you've rubbed the wrong person the wrong way or haven't rubbed the right people the right way. You can take a number of steps, but first be on the lookout for and quickly recognize the key indicators that you could be entering a troubling situation or are already in trouble. The sooner you recognize these signs, the sooner you can try to reconcile the situation.

Events happening within the company

- There is corporate pressure for "profit now." This usually means that the company is less likely to invest in personnel who look for improvements that take time—like you.

- There is consolidation of departments. This usually means that the company wants to do more of what they do now with fewer people, especially boat-rockers like you.
- Company awards and recognition are consistency given to low-impact players who are clearly management favorites—not like you.
- Personal or departmental silos are tolerated and may receive preferential treatment over others.
- Executive presentations avoid accountability for issues that are negatively impacting the company, such as poor leadership and missed opportunities.

Personal events that indicate that a visionary is not appreciated in the company or department, or by his boss

- The disposable visionary is left out of meetings.
- The disposable visionary is left out of the process when new hires are made in the department.
- The disposable visionary's boss has less time for him, either in one-on-one meetings or with patience to listen to the employee in group meetings.
- Projects or opportunities that impact multiple departments are given to others to handle, not to the disposable visionary.
- Personal reviews center less on achievements and more on why the disposable visionary isn't making nice in the area of company politics.

When you see these conditions, it's time to act. Uncomfortable as it may be, it is time to put your own needs first. Even if you are not sure you want to play the game, you need to at least understand the situation and take steps to regain your footing. After that, you can take the time to assess whether or not the long-term fight is worth the effort.

Remember, you can't change the company from the street. You need to make changes in yourself that will realign you with what the company wants and to convey your commitment to contribute on common terms . . . though most of them will be their terms. The following actions are recommended for regaining trust and identifying how to show your commitment to contribute to the company:

1. Have a heart-to-heart conversation with your boss. This should always start with your desire to contribute to the company. From there, you should express both your own frustration and your perception of the company's frustration. Clarify the reasons you were hired and the freedom you perceived to pursue the goals that you

understood the company set for you. Try to get a sense of where you are disconnecting from those goals and how you can work together to correct the situation while still trying to pursue breakthroughs.

2. If your boss is the problem or is inaccessible, consider meeting with his or her boss to discuss your disappointment concerning your own inability to perform like you want. Don't use that time to complain about your boss. Provide assurances that you want to help make your boss successful, make the company successful, and make your customers successful, as you were supposedly hired to do, but need some guidance on how to work more effectively. This shows that you are looking at the big picture, that you want to be a team player, and that you recognize that some issues are present. Remember, this is not a time to complain about your boss. Take responsibility for any misunderstanding, and ask for guidance on how to work better with a key person in the company. If this creates a rift with your supervisor, it was already there before you talked.

The above steps show you are committed to the company and care about staying. If they don't secure additional time in your current position, they may at least open up the opportunity to get a second chance somewhere else in the company. This leads to the third step.

3. Share your insights with your champion, and get his opinion. His insights reflect his understanding of the company and should guide you toward other steps. Most importantly, don't be timid about asking him for help and asking to work together if possible. He understands your dilemma and should perceive the value you bring.

Finally, be aware of your own feelings and the effect they are having on your attitude and performance. Chapter 11 goes into more detail on the dangers of pessimism and obvious frustration, but for now, it is important to accept the fact that openly negative and destructive attitudes will undermine any chance for radical change. New ideas and radical proposals always come under heavy scrutiny. They can't afford to be weighed down by accusations or concerns about an employee's personal behavior apart from passionate pursuit of what is best for the company. For this reason, focus on effectively channeling frustrations into initiatives that will further the cause of change, not spread unproductive negativity.

When you know that what you are doing is right, it is hard to compromise. However, it is also important to recognize that sometimes you have to compromise before you can improvise. Hold to your values and your dreams. Don't waver from your focus, but understand that the more people you can get on your side, including your boss and peers, the greater the chance your ideas will come to fruition.

We may honor those who die on their swords. But they don't contribute much to the next battle.

So, what does this mean?

It all boils down to one simple question: "Am I sure that I am making the right people (i.e., the company, my boss, their boss, others of influence, and the customer) successful? And are my ideas positioned to be perceived that way?" When innovations are understood, analyzed, and appreciated by the right people in the right way, then DVS employees have the greatest opportunity to make positive contributions to an organization. It's all a matter of methods, measurement, and a message geared to the most important audiences.

GEORGE S. PATTON

"I JUST WANT TO END THE WAR. . ."

General George S. Patton never suffered a major defeat in the Second World War. He was regarded by the enemy as our greatest weapon. He foresaw the potential Russian threat. He believed in never fighting for the same ground twice, and he would not suffer the political and human costs of waiting while our allies caught up. Yet he was relieved of duty twice and denied greater opportunities . . . due to political missteps.

Early in his career, Patton saw the future of mechanized firepower when he assumed command of America's first tank operations in 1917. During WWII, the successes of the German tank blitzkriegs placed new importance on armored warfare that Patton seized with a single-minded passion.

Once in Europe, Patton's tank units blazed a trail of important victories:

- He led the successful invasion of Sicily, marching to Messina, which opened the Mediterranean to Allied shipping and led to the resignation of Benito Mussolini.
- He led Operation Torch, which secured the defeat of German tank commander Erwin Rommel in North Africa, four months after American forces had been soundly defeated there.

(Continued)

- He led the liberation of France and, in the process, destroyed the German 7th Army, capturing more than 100,000 German soldiers at the Falaise-Argentan Gap.
- He saved Allied forces from a surprise rear attack in Ardennes by diverting his France campaign 90 degrees north to defeat the German forces at the Battle of the Bulge.
- He crossed the Rhine River and secured victories in central Germany, Northern Bavaria, and Czechoslovakia, actions key to the final German surrender. His German advance ended only when Stalin protested Patton's crossing into Czechoslovakia.

In addition to many other key victories in the liberation of Europe, the general was also part of Eisenhower's planning force for the Normandy invasion.

Patton also understood the value of politics when dealing with the enemy and aligning allies to his cause. Following the capture of Casablanca in French Morocco, his use of diplomacy gained Arab help in destroying German communication lines. He then obtained support of pro-Axis Spanish Morocco leaders by inviting them to review his troops, which was all they needed to get the message.

But Patton did not give the same careful attention to Allied politics. His failures resulted from a simple belief that winning the war was more important than taking the time to play political games. He was outspoken about ineffective British battle plans for the capture of Sicily that allowed German forces to escape following his victory. He was indignant at soldiers who were hospitalized for battle fatigue. In two instances, he slapped soldiers as a display to the wounded that honor came with dedication and sacrifice. He made public comments about potential Russian threats. And during his campaigns, he obtained fuel and supplies to maintain his pursuit of the German army without proper approvals.

As a result, Patton received numerous reprimands and was relieved of duty. Three days after defeating Rommel, he was relieved of command because of his disputes with the British. The slapping incidents cost him command of the 3rd Army after the victory in Sicily, and he was demoted to playing decoy during the invasion of Normandy. His comments on the Russians and his advocacy for use of ex-Nazis to retain order in postwar Germany resulted in his reassignment to an administrative position rather than the field command in the Pacific he had eagerly sought.

A controversial commander, Patton nonetheless proved himself masterful in overcoming his opponents on the battlefield, but he failed to recognize the weapon that would give him the greatest long-term firepower: the support of his superiors.[1,2,3]

Chapter 9

Four Corporate Cultures: Maximizing Your Impact in Each

Before you shave off your corners, find out if the hole is round or square

The concept of an overnight mail delivery service is interesting and well formed, but in order to earn better than a C, the idea must be feasible.

Unidentified Yale professor to Fred Smith, founder of Federal Express

The guidelines in Chapter 7 are recommended for any visionary in any cultural environment. They create the basis for greater integration and have the potential not only for longer tenure, but also to influence other employees as well the organization.

But in any organization, there will also be some cultural issues that the DVS employee should consider. Her actions and attitude for survival will be affected by the type of organization culture in which she works and how she adjusts her vision to the style of the company. She must recognize what they feel is important and how they organize around it.

Almost all companies believe that they have productive and exciting environments. They believe that they are unique in what they do and how they achieve their goals. This is what makes it difficult to institute change. The emperor is often the last to see that he has no clothes.

But contrary to the unique image companies may have of themselves; there are really just a few key differences that characterize the working culture. From a DVS employee's viewpoint, the issues of culture center around two issues:

Where the company's true vision is centered (i.e., its true focus
on what is important)
and
The philosophy of how to run the company to get there.

In its basic form, and forgetting all the buzzwords and organizational development introspective, it all comes down to whether the company's most pressing focus is on profit or growth and whether its means relies on control or empowerment. This results in four categories of culture that the visionary should consider when looking at how to fit in and contribute (Figure 9.1):

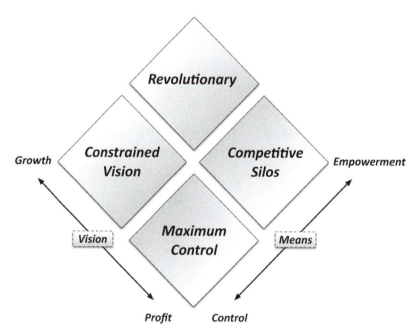

Figure 9.1   The Four Corporate Cultures

1. The **Maximum Control** environment, which focuses on profit and high control of how things are done;
2. The **Competitive Silo** environment, which empowers employees to contribute, but focus on maximizing profit;

3. The **Constrained Vision** environment, which seeks growth but has high control on how employees will contribute; and

4. The **Revolutionary** environment, which focuses on growth and empowers employees to contribute in their most effective manner.

Examining each will help the DVS employee to define his environment and the steps that can effectively enable him or her to function and contribute to the fullest level.

The **Maximum Control** environment tends to be inwardly focused. While it considers customer needs, it seeks to maximize its current profit, which may come at some sacrifice to how it serves the long-term needs or how it regards the importance of long-term loyalty of its customers or employees. Internally, it has heavy controls on how this is achieved. This may not mean that there is no flexibility, but there are clear guidelines. It may mean that one department takes priority in deciding what is done. It may mean that investment spending is limited to certain areas. The message sent from this culture is that each employee can contribute, but only as long as they acknowledge very clear guidelines, priorities, and political hierarchies.

In this environment, the DVS employee might also consider managing himself or herself with the following:

Set your own pace, but acknowledge the company line. Find ways to align with what is important to the dominant person, idea, or department; make a difference where the company is focused. If they look at ROI, ensure that your innovations can contribute to a documented greater return. If the sales force is the dominant department, find ways to make them dependent on you with concepts that directly aid them in ways that they feel comfortable implementing.

Establish singles and doubles before you start swinging for home runs. Look at enhancements to existing strategies or operations. They are looking for profit, so focus on increasing revenue or decreasing cost in the ways they are currently doing business. They are not interested in long-term investments, including you, so you have to earn the right to pursue bigger programs later.

Lead with the economic benefits. Quantify any recommendations with short-term payoffs, and allow others to discover that these short-term payoffs are also designed in such a way that they are creating a greater overall effect as they work together. The challenge is not just what the "big win" can be; it is also how to create an incremental development process where each progressive step also provides its own impact.

Consider planting an idea and letting someone else, preferably in the controlling group, sponsor it. The quickest way to get an idea killed in this culture is to run into opposition from the area in control. Excessive passion about an outside idea will threaten those in control. Offer your help to see it through. Its success and yours establish your own credibility and may spread to your department and your boss, which is a good thing. It could even break the control and form the basis for a more productive environment.

The **Competitive Silo** culture also focuses on internal profit, but it offers more independence in achieving that goal. However, with that independence comes a strong inside competitive nature. This is the result of the emergence of lots of independent silos, each striving for long-term existence and trying to gain some prominence in an effort to become the focus of a maximum control group that may evolve if the organization shifts to growth. Therefore, there is little integration or corporate innovation that will allow the best ideas to come to the front. Seniority is a strong player, and there will be recognition through preferential treatment of some individuals and departments, but it is a fluid seniority. "What have you done for me lately?" is still a large criterion. Not all areas and ideas are considered equal.

To survive and still make an impact in this environment, the DVS employee should do the following:

Take the lead in integration. Initiative is part of the culture, and dominant players have not emerged. Look for the win-win opportunities to create solutions that leverage multiple strengths and impact multiple departments. If you seek out other DVS employees, ensure that a measurable impact on profit comes from your efforts.

Look for ways to make your department, and especially your boss, well recognized. Your focus is on effective change, and if you can become indispensable to your boss, you will have a greater opportunity to create that impact. As you know, it doesn't matter if you get the credit, but in this case, you do want your boss to recognize your value.

Find out where your boss's boss is applying pressure. It may be a key result, or it could involve politics. You want to create a success that matters to those who can give you more latitude later for the things that really matter. Win where it is important to them, and you'll get the chance for greater impact later.

Form indirect alliances with people in competing silos or with third parties; for example, established consultants who have access to several silos. These people can be an excellent source of information and can be instant allies if cross-silo committees are formed. This allows you to get in on the ground floor of the key initiatives and to ensure that they are looking at the greatest potential, with your influence.

The **Constrained Vision** environment can be one of the most frustrating for the disposable visionary. The company talks growth, expects growth, and promises growth, yet puts constraints on the organization's ability to achieve it. As with the Maximum Control culture, the areas of control can come from process, priorities, or predominant departments or functions. Yet the company seeks change, but within limitations.

To survive in this type of organization without going crazy, an effective DVS employee might consider the following:

Get a definition of the guidelines. In a control culture, there are boundaries and limits that you need to define. However, once you clarify those, you can use them as the basis for stretching and pushing the envelope. The key to your success in breaking new ground will be to find innovative ways to change the ways the organization works inside the box, not outside it.

Identify and understand the key areas of control. Finding a champion in one of these areas will be very helpful in this culture. He or she might give you a seasoned perception of how to play the game as well as providing you with credibility under their approval. Getting input and support from influential people will gain you greater acceptance when presenting your efforts.

Find out how the most important changes have occurred in the past. Who led the charge, what was the process for the proposal and the implementation, and who made the decisions? In most cases, they will come from focused approaches, well thought out and with limited disruption within the organization. As such, you want to avoid being chairman of the dumb idea club. The controlling character of this culture will put great constraints on ideas—even those that can revolutionize the company. But remember, those in this culture say they want growth, but only under control, and that means limitations on implementation and thus on what they will consider. It will be better to be chairman of the common sense club, with a scrupulous review of ideas that make sense and move the organization forward, but with little risk and much up-front evaluation and revision.

Try to create or define a process for evaluating ideas. There will be a lot of reasons why ideas won't work in this culture. Constraining priorities and control become more dominant than vision. Therefore, ideas need an internal champion process that identifies and automatically supports ideas that meet agreed-upon criteria. In doing so, the company will also end up spelling out very clear priorities for what it considers to be most important. This process and the result can help make a culture into a more dynamic, priority-focused organization rather than a risk-averse one.

Finally, consider the impact of the negative sell. When cultures are at conflict with themselves, they often need to look in the mirror when making evaluations. When they realize the constraints they are putting on themselves, then they may be open to change. As such, it is sometimes very successful to introduce radical ideas with the follow-up statement, "Of course, this might not work here." The reaction is likely to be, "Why not?" and management, accused of being non-visionary, may work very hard to disprove the assertion and, in the process, sell themselves on the idea. Be sure you get in on the implementation, to ensure that your vision is maintained and that the political constraints are held to a minimum.

The **Revolutionary** culture should be a disposable visionary's dream. It recognizes the need for ongoing improvement and innovation and understands that revolutions come from passion. The organization is visionary, yet there will be a keen sense of costs and investments. You can't change the world from bankruptcy very often. The organization should recognize that a focused revolution requires an openness to overthrow, but you want to overthrow ideas, not people. A successful revolutionary culture requires direction but maintains passion—not for change for change's sake, but instead for progress and innovation.

While this culture sounds great, it also comes with some special responsibility for the DVS employee. They will not just look for change; they will want very focused, thought-out, and integrated innovations.

The demand for change can be in some ways as frustrating as resistance to change. In some organizations, the mandate for progress and change takes precedence over clear vision and direction. The focus for change can be a moving target, or like trying to put form on a handful of Jell-O. Too much change can prevent any one concept from hardening to a point where it can be measured or used as the foundation for future enhancements. In other organizations, the desire for change has its limits, and in the other extreme, things finally come to a halt so the current design can be evaluated, and change is resisted . . . even those innovations that build on what is important to the organization.

To deal with such a culture and the possible variations within it, the DVS employee should consider the following strategies within the **Revolutionary** organization:

Go to extremes to bring in others throughout the development process. Because change is such a cultural mandate, integration will be expected. The impactful evidence of teamwork and innovations that cross departments will carry the greatest weight. Being a solo maverick is not a desired image in this environment. Part of the program is the openness to leverage and empower others. Use and display it.

Be flexible. Your ability to work in changing teams will be crucial. Be open to personalities. Challenge others, but also help to develop them, and use them in the formulation and execution of what will achieve the greatest contribution.

Be disciplined in your process; in fact, take the lead if the organization lacks a clear planning and evaluation process. As in the Constrained Vision culture, one of the challenges will be ensuring that the right ideas are identified and developed. Also, be sure the planning process includes long-term measurements. This ensures recognition that many programs need to be evaluated over time, and it helps establish longevity. How can you measure impact if it changes before it has time to be effective? Thus, a measurement standard helps to prevent premature distortion by requiring some measurements.

If necessary, recognize and understand when good is good enough. As an organization tires of constant change, it will want to step back— sometimes out of appropriate design, to give things a chance to take effect, and sometimes just out of inability to keep up or to adopt the discipline of creating an effective evaluation process that enables ongoing, focused change. When this happens, the DVS employee must step back and stop pushing on the next generation. Don't strive for perfection. Let good enough be good enough. However, this is also the time to recognize the need for the guidelines and standards mentioned. Concentrate your efforts on getting the organization able and ready to resume at a faster, more focused, yet more engaged pace.

As these examples show, change can come from within an organization. Just as a company can grow by focusing on what is important to the customer, so can DVS employees help a company grow by first focusing on and acknowledging what is important to the organization.

Cultures can change, but they have to change based on what they are, as well as what they should be. Start with what works (or what they think works) for the organization, and leverage that foundation. To reach a vision down the road, you'll need to recognize that you are also walking from a foundation—and you need to use it as the starting point in order to reach your destination. But with a visionary's ability to focus on creating the greatest potential, it can be done.

So what does this mean?

You can make any company's culture work to your advantage, though some will be easier than others. Identify the culture, and then look at the organization's written mission and vision as well as its unofficial power base, or who makes the real decisions. One of the biggest challenges will be to reconcile these factors, but when that is accomplished, you will have an unbeatable combination for achieving change.

WOODROW WILSON

THE CONTROLLING FACTION: WHEN COLLEGE TRUSTEES CAN'T BE TRUSTED

If you want to make enemies, try to change something.

Woodrow Wilson

A true visionary, Woodrow Wilson initiated sweeping changes as president of Princeton University, successfully managed America's victory in the first war on a global basis, presided over America's postwar emergence, and proposed the prototype for the United Nations. A leader with little political patience, he was fired by Princeton University and was unsuccessful in the political bickering with his own Congress over the League of Nations, designed to spread democracy throughout the world.

Joining the Princeton faculty in 1890, Wilson quickly became one of the most popular lecturers on campus and was selected as the university's 13th president in 1902. By 1906, he was at the height of his popularity. Students, alumni, faculty, and trustees all enthusiastically endorsed his contributions and his leadership. He was considered the indispensable man for Princeton. During this time, Wilson created key hallmarks that have impacted the university ever since.

The first non-Presbyterian minister to serve as president, Wilson established the university's famous precept system, where professors conduct small, more intimate sessions with students; expanded the area of scientific studies to complement liberal arts; created a graduate school; hired the first Jewish and Roman Catholic faculty members; and established Princeton's first endowment.

Wilson also envisioned a more cohesive student body, built on the concept of undergraduate colleges and known as the Quad Plan. This plan consolidated the upper-class eating clubs, which were fraternity-like off-campus nonresidential facilities where juniors and seniors had their meals and whose membership was based on invitation, with selected dormitories and faculty members to create a more cohesive and unified student body. As Wilson saw it, it would replace a system that sharply divided the students with one that incorporated the best of all the original elements, while at the same time creating a more unified, supportive, and engaging environment. And incidentally, the system is currently popular at Harvard and Yale, among other institutions.

Unfortunately, while this plan had immense social and intellectual potential for the students, Wilson did not have the political patience to move slowly. As such, when alumni of the clubs misinterpreted his vision, as misstated in the June 25, 1907, *New York Times* headline "Wilson to Abolish Clubs at Princeton," he found himself on the defensive. He had not identified the controlling faction—in this case, alumni—who eagerly defended their "loyalty to their respective clubs with little recognition or a readiness to appreciate the goals that he was promulgating and endeavoring to achieve."[1] Despite numerous reports that supported Wilson's perception of social splits, the trustees refused to address needed changes to the system, and Wilson was forced to resign in 1910. His eight-year tenure was the shortest in the history of Princeton since 1766.

Chapter 10

How to Manage a DVS Employee

Stoke the flame without extinguishing the spark

Only the mediocre are always at their best.

Jean Giraudaoux

Managers, peers, and human resources personnel often ask how to deal with DVS employees. The question should not be, "How do I deal with the DVS employee?" The question should be, "How can I best leverage the DVS employee? How should I use, learn from, and even exploit the DVS employee?" This is not a situation to address; it is an opportunity to pursue. To that end, this chapter is addressed specifically to those who work with DVS employees.

WHY YOU NEED VISIONARY EMPLOYEES

DVS employees have the characteristics that most companies need. They also have the characteristics that most companies even pursue: talent, drive, and the desire to achieve. They focus these traits on the things that can matter and that can make a real difference. In contrast, many PAR employees take those same traits and, by focusing on themselves, end up with self-promotion, personal agendas, and control of others. If you can leverage the passion and vision of DVS employees in a manner that reignites the energy and talents of the rest of the company, the results can be dramatic.

Not surprisingly, if their activity is encouraged and if they last long enough, DVS employees can make other employees more successful, including their managers. In fact, an added benefit of DVS employment is the opportunity to evaluate management's ability to leverage and enhance the talent of their staff. When DVS employees are terminated, it is not only time to evaluate the culture that created the misfit, but perhaps it is also an indication that it is time to evaluate the management talent that failed to integrate them and their passion constructively into the organization.

As iron sharpens iron, visionaries can bring out the best in a manager. The skills, insights, motivation, and accountability that are necessary to guide and focus the DVS employee are characteristics of the best managers and executives. Developing these attributes will enhance the performance of all employees.

Chapter 6 presented the concept of the DVS Coach—the generalist who also can oversee and inspire the best in others. It is exciting to see the full potential of a team come together, but it takes an individual with the combination of being able to see the possibilities, understanding the political obstacles, encouraging individual talents, and developing ways to pave the road to integrate them into the culture and protect them from not only antagonists but even from themselves. More politically dangerous than herding cats, it is more like corralling loose cannons. Let's face it, a disposable visionary is hardly an easy bargain in the fun-to-manage department, but every so often, a boss comes along who can bring out the best in him or her. He or she offers a calming effect similar to the feeling you get when someone actually listens to your ideas. Consider the following example of such a visionary whisperer.

HAL'S STORY

Hal was a VP in a surreal little corner of the sprawling corporate hydra that was MacroBankUS in the eighties. The department was originally designed to bring in a group of mavericks, diverse in backgrounds and sought for their new, innovative ideas. Looking at their eventual careers, they were also a group of budding superstars:

1. An operations wizard who later became one the 50 most powerful women in banking in the world
2. A instructional guru who rolled out the first IRA programs and changed the way banking staff sold products and related to their customers
3. A PR innovator who brought national recognition to a regional enterprise and took community involvement to a level of indispensability
4. An advertising maverick who later pioneered the use of direct response television for package goods companies
5. A product manager who stopped looking at "what we've got" and always looked at "what could be," thus creating dozens of breakthrough financial products that we take for granted today

Truly, Hal had assembled a corporate island of misfit pros, and the company would not have missed them if they had been exorcized and replaced by employees with traditional square profiles to fit in the traditional square holes.

But Hal recognized that his job was to encourage the talent while protecting their backs. He used his own visionary skills to recognize bold, new, and big ideas and always asked, "How can we break through to the next level and change the playing field in banking?" Then he instituted failsafe processes that gave structure and internal order to the group's passion. In his department, Process with a capital "P" was king. He required detailed task lists outlining the desired end result and the steps they would take to get there. This meant interim approvals with key players and regular check-ins. He also required that his staff develop the necessary personal relationships with management, peers, support staff, and the sales teams. This was critical to achieving trust and eliminating potential adversaries. Finally, he made sure that the more mundane but expected activities in marketing, product development, training, and data management were highly visible. This ensured that others saw ongoing work that established daily value. It also provided a perspective for the staff to integrate the future with the present.

Hal knew that fueling the fire in his staff also required intentional protection—to prevent others from putting out the fire, because after all, fire can be threatening. To do so, he put his own job on the line, and if unnecessary obstacles were thrown up by other departments, he would dash down the hallway to the offending department head's office, close the door, and emerge 20 minutes later with the barrier to progress removed.

He created a tough, adrenaline-pumping, energizing culture. His visionaries had plenty of challenges, disagreements, and obstacles, but they didn't have to watch their backs. Hal was there for that. They blazed new territory and reveled in it. In two short years, they created and marketed the first home equity credit line, pioneered data-driven sales at the retail level, invented new concepts in customer loyalty programs, introduced time-sensitive investment promotions, broke new ground in integrating securities and investments into retail banking, and expanded traditional mortgage products with more flexible terms and conditions. Their innovations set the standards for the industry for the next decade.

During his time, Hal created not only a great culture, but also great people who were confident in pursuing new ideas and in supporting their peers. They put up with the steps necessary for their own protection, because they knew that their boss was daily putting his career on the line for them, and if it became necessary, they would have put theirs on the line for him as well.

So how do you leverage the skills of the DVS employee without going crazy? With the proper attention, a manager can easily maximize the potential of DVS employees, make heroes of them to the organization, and, in fact, make a hero of himself. All it takes is concentration in four key areas that not only will direct and encourage the DVS employee to perform up to the potential you sought when you hired him, but also will ensure that he is aligned with the key goals of the organization.

As we just mentioned, these same four areas of focus also characterize the most effective management approaches in dealing with any employee. However, the lack of their execution by management becomes more obvious with DVS employees, who will go off on their own to contribute in some manner whether they receive effective management involvement or not.

The four areas are easily remembered due to their acronym. They can best be summarized as reflecting management with a VIEW. The four letters of VIEW represent the four areas of concentration that compose the most effective management approach to enhance visionary, and other, employees:

V. **VISION** must be established and communicated to support a clear understanding of the department's role in the overall scheme of things.

I. **INTEGRATE** the passion, innovation, and ideology of the DVS employee within your department and throughout the organization.

E. **ENHANCE** the employee's talent, passion, and pursuit of breakthrough innovations. Take a talented employee, and make him even better.

W. **WATCH** for ways to prevent the internal obstacles that stymie employees' performance and support.

We will take each of these management initiatives and explore its implications in more detail.

VISION: Establish, communicate, and support a clear understanding of the vision of your organization and department.

Implementing and communicating a vision goes beyond reciting a mission statement. It requires a clear understanding of how your customer regards your organization, how you are becoming indispensable to him, and in daily terms, how you measure progress in your development to serve the customer. The DVS employee has a passion to meet those objectives but needs clarity on what is expected and how success will be defined. How do you measure success? Exactly what does your mission look like when it achieves the absolute highest level possible? How do you know when you have created a preemptive position in the market? These are crucial direction for any employee but especially for the disposable visionary, since he is personally committed to finding the most effective way to achieve your vision.

Therefore, in conveying your vision, you should provide the following:

1. Clearly align the DVS employee with a detailed understanding of what matters most to the organization and how your organization wants to meet the most important needs of your customer. There is no room for fluff in this process. The DVS employee needs to see that his role is important in creating the greatest impact and has breakthrough importance in what and how you deliver your product or service. For the most effective alignment, establish clear measurements of how the organization evaluates its success in achieving its vision. This provides the DVS employee with the ability to focus his passion and innovative spirit against a clear objective. Very importantly, it should also allow management to provide the DVS employee with the freedom to pursue that vision with out-of-the-box thinking and new approaches unhampered by excessive constraints and obstacles. Managers should also feel comfortable that their direction will result in work performed that will meet clear measurements that are meaningful to the customer and within the corporate goals. There should be no frustration, only pleasant surprises, when solutions are raised that effectively meet your own clear criteria.
2. Establish and communicate clear and challenging standards within the vision. Set the highest goals and standards possible in achieving the vision. Don't settle for sales or retention goals when you could be striving for preemptive strategies that lock customers in. DVS employees provide a resource that lets you set higher standards and

stretch your own dreams. Let your DVS employee help you reach for your dreams. In your goal development, be sure to create a specific vision for your own department as well as following that of the organization. DVS employees can handle multiple expectations. They also understand reasonable constraints if they are well explained. Explain the playing rules, but also allow them to swing for the fences.

3. Be patient with the DVS employee concerning the opportunities and obstacles in reaching the full potential of your vision. He will question. He will provide ideas that may not be fully developed. He will push. An effective DVS manager should be a good listener, understanding the frustrations of the DVS employee and providing clear direction for the pursuit of innovation and impact. Too many managers try to resolve conflict too quickly, and ideas and passion die. Show the employee that you value ideas and that you will take the time to look for the potential. It is also important that you take the role of "giant killer" in getting rid of obstacles that prevent ideas and innovation from developing. To do so, you need to understand the opportunity you are fighting for as well as the obstacles you may need to remove.

4. Recognize that vision is achieved through the management of talent, not through control, processes, or politics. This means using your listening and discernment skills carefully and frequently. Identify the DVS employee. They should now be easy to see. Recognize their DVS style and how they may be most impactful to your organization. As with any employee, examine how to leverage their strengths rather than just changing their perceived weaknesses or differences. Give them focus, and let them surprise you. Your vision, in the true and greatest sense of the word, now has a greater chance of becoming a reality.

INTEGRATION: Take the necessary steps to integrate the passion, innovation, and ideology of the DVS employee within your department and throughout the organization.

DVS employees bring a passion, excitement, and sense of commitment that should not be isolated. Managers have a responsibility to leverage these employees' talents for the greatest contribution in the company. Their effective integration will result in more effective productivity and excitement within the organization. Effective integration should include attention to the following:

1. Assimilate the activities of DVS employees within the organization. This not only means to physically integrate DVS employees with other DVS and non-DVS employees. It also means to find ways to integrate

their innovation, drive, and passion within the culture. Teams including DVS employees have greater potential for breakthrough thinking. Recognizing the different DVS styles and combining them creates the potential for more insightful solutions. Combined with other employees, the DVS solutions may address some of the political issues raised by other employees to address unfortunate, but real, internal obstacles. The implementation of new ideas will be easier when more employees have had the opportunity to participate in their development and the identification and resolution of potential issues.

2. Accept—even encourage—conflict. The best ideas come from aggressive challenges and confrontation. While they should not get personal, they also should not be avoided or quickly resolved. As a manager, you should create the ground rules for such confrontations, but they should be a natural result of the pursuit of breakthrough ideas and revolutionary thinking. In creating a culture that best leverages conflict, realize that management's role is not always to resolve conflict. Greater solutions, teamwork, and an ongoing supportive culture result when employees are provided clear expectations and goals but left to work out the differences themselves.

3. Find and formalize ways to encourage targeted out-of-box thinking geared toward your vision. Identify the key areas that your vision touches. They will be more than simply creating the best product. They should include desires for measured improvement in service innovation, employee motivation, process improvement, and mutual support, among other areas. In short, they should address the elements that are touched by all four DVS styles. Dream for what could be, and integrate the culture to stimulate your DVS employees and others to help achieve those stretch goals and visionary dreams. Good managers go beyond asking for ideas; they create a process for recognizing, managing, and evaluating those ideas. It takes special insight and vision. But it provides your DVS employees with the focus they need and creates a guideline for non-DVS employees to begin a more productive ideation process. This is one of the special benefits of DVS employees: it allows management to raise and articulate their vision, often at a higher level than they would normally set.

4. Hold all your employees to the stretch standards you want to achieve. Goals and visions must be accompanied by measurements. You need to get serious about their achievement. Both DVS and non-DVS employees must be held accountable if you are to stretch your achievements for what could be. This means giving clear standards that in turn keep your DVS employees focused on pursuing what is important. But if it becomes clear that the standards and measurements are

not impacting what is most important, then drop them. Visionaries love challenges. Provided the opportunity to pursue the dream comes with minimal obstacles and constraints, they will come up with the ways to achieve the goals you set. But just as you expect them to meet your standards, you also have the responsibility to help remove any internal obstacles—and especially the political ones.

ENHANCEMENT: Enhance the employee's talent, passion, and pursuit of breakthrough innovations.

The most important role of management is not just to leverage talent, but also to develop it. DVS employees, like all employees, appreciate the chance to develop their skills. Like all employees, they also grow through constructive criticism, guidance, recognition, and additional opportunities to contribute to the company in its vision. As we have discussed, the different styles of DVS employees reflect different talents and will result in different approaches, not only in how they solve problems, but also in how they present their solutions. Enhancing their performance will come from being attentive to their personal strengths and talents and the ways in which you evaluate and recognize their ideas and productivity. Enhancing performance, then, can be reduced to simply focusing on the potential end result, which is a combination of a more satisfied customer, a more productive organization, and a more empowered and talented employee.

1. Don't focus on the details while evaluating ideas or recommendations. While the devil may be in the details, you must avoid concentrating on why ideas aren't perfect and, instead, look at the potential. If you want to guide DVS employees to ensure that their focus is aligned with your vision and to head off any corporate issues, then you will want to see works in progress. This means you will be presented with many concepts, which may not always be thought through. Remember, the Creator/Engager may not be as attentive to the detail issues as the Mechanic/Designer. The greatest opportunity lies in simply presenting issues and allowing the DVS employee to solve them, preferably with the help of other DVS or non-DVS employees. A common management error is pulling the plug too early. This not only kills many great ideas before they have a chance to develop, but it also begins to kill the incentive and motivation of employees.

2. Remember that DVS employees are not concerned with their self-promotion. This means that management may not always recognize the contribution they are making. Contrary to many corporate cultures, effective management of visionaries should encourage the selfless approach of DVS employees. Putting pressure on employees

for self-promotion undermines the focus of the employee on what can move the company, not himself, forward. Sometimes, it will take special effort by management to uncover the depth of the contribution and the potential from works in progress. However, such efforts not only create additional stimulus for the DVS employee, but they also become very evident and motivating to other employees, sending the message that performance, not politics or promotion, is what matters.

3. Provide the freedom to perform. In enhancing and building on employees with passion and focus, managers must create a culture of empowerment. This comes not only from clear direction and standards but also through an environment that excites employees and allows them to step out. Such an environment should provide eight key freedoms:

Freedom to fail. Not every idea is perfect; not every effort will come to a final delivery. Sometimes external obstacles become prohibitive to the organization; sometimes internal issues, rightly or wrongly, take priority.

Freedom to provide ideas in progress. Don't overly criticize initial concepts or focus on what is missing; encourage the potential while identifying issues that will have to be addressed. Give ideas (as well as the employee) a chance to develop to their fullest impact.

Freedom to speak and question openly. Let them know it's permissible to disagree with other people, departments, ideas, traditions, and politics. Accept the risk and the potential that comes from constructive conflict. If necessary, set the ground rules for conflict, but don't restrict its potential.

Freedom to think out of the box at a higher level. Don't place undue restrictions, traditional approaches, or areas of comfort in the way of potential breakthroughs, and continue to offer new challenges as a reward for previous achievements.

Freedom to be accountable. Set standards, and give the employee the responsibility to meet them in the most effective ways possible.

Freedom to do what is right. Encourage employees to hold to their ethics, to challenge others in ethical issues, to support others over themselves, and to give others credit.

Freedom to develop their own talents to the fullest. Allow DVS employees to pursue passions that help them build on their talents and that support their dedication to create innovative approaches and influence.

Freedom from excessive freedom. Provide a focus of direction. If there are real obstacles or roadblocks, clearly identify them up front.

4. Judge against standards. You have set standards. You have even established stretch goals for the DVS employee. Now hold yourself to them as well. Remove your personal judgments, and evaluate your employees, their ideas, their productivity, and their behavior against those standards. Are they meeting the criteria you established? If so, let the small things go. If not, then identify why and provide the direction, refinement, or input that will enable the DVS employees to regain their focus and pursue the proper direction with renewed passion and dedication.

WATCH: Carefully watch for opportunities to leverage individual DVS talent most effectively, as well as for ways to prevent internal obstacles that stymie their performance and support.

The final key to leveraging DVS employees is through observation. This is not only in what you see happening around the organization and with the employee; it means keeping an eye on your own actions as well.

1. First, recognize the specific talents of the employee. Which of the four DVS styles fits each of your visionary staff members? How can you leverage those skills most effectively toward your vision for the organization and your department? How can you match individuals and teams that best utilize their talents and passion? And in matching them, watch for interaction with other DVS and non-DVS employees, and support the final goal.
2. Second, watch your own words and actions. As outlined in Chapter 5, DVS employees will not interpret politically obscure messages. Say what you mean, and mean what you say. Don't keep quiet about what you want. This will hold you more accountable for your words and actions, and it will create the focus you desire. It will also ensure that you clearly outline the standards you want to establish. Stand firm in your convictions, not only in dealing directly with the DVS employee, but also in how you hold others to those same standards.
3. Watch for opportunities to be a part of the DVS employee's passion. You should be seen as his biggest supporter. Set up meetings, and listen. Find out his thinking and how his vision complements yours. This allows you not only to guide the process appropriately, but also to provide your valuable insights and suggestions to enhance his activity. Do expect blunt answers and challenges, but take them as a desire for improvement, not a personal affront.
4. Watch for ways to provide political guidance. No culture is without its politics. Some are just more explosive than others in that respect. The long-term success of the DVS employee will depend on how the

organization leverages his potential and on how well the visionary adapts to the culture of the organization. Identify the crucial political issues that the employee needs to accept and adopt into his approach. Be practical in what is important, and realize that excessive politics can get in the way of innovative productivity. Be specific in what the culture demands, yet also be open to taking on the organization yourself if you observe that the political climate has elements that restrict the full pursuit of the vision of the organization and your department. The greatest contribution management can make is to get permission and clear the road to allow their staff to excel toward the greatest contributions. Such efforts will also create greater openness for all of your employees, and especially visionaries, to share their activities and make you a greater part of the success.

5. Finally, executives should watch the managers of DVS employees. They need to be given permission to support these potential superstars. So often, the talent we hire does not contribute as we hoped. And they are discarded. However, we must ensure that they are receiving the nurturing and given the vision, freedom, and opportunity to produce to their fullest potential. Plants cannot grow if they are constrained by small pots. DVS employees cannot produce if they are constrained by managers with small minds.

The same issues that the manager of a visionary needs to display are also required of their management. To enable managers to best manage, their management teams need to provide them with a clear vision and understanding of what is expected, along with the freedom to pursue it without excessive control or politics. They need to hold them to clear stretch goals that force them to find ways to get the most out of their staff and peers. When there is not enough conflict, when there are not sufficient innovations, these managers need to be held accountable . . . while given the same opportunities to function with minimum restrictions and obstacles.

While the above descriptions of the four areas of management with a VIEW have detailed how to manage a DVS employee, it is also important to recognize the special impact and issues when a DVS employee is part of management. All of the above issues are the same and even amplified in this situation. DVS managers will be searching for ways to motivate and stimulate greater thinking among their staff and peers. As such, they may appear to be less involved in the day-to-day issues. They are looking at the big picture more than politics. They will promote their people more than themselves. They will deal with results more than paperwork. They will challenge their fellow executives and put them on the spot. And if they don't perceive the greatest potential in the company line, they'll implement and motivate a following for a vision of their own.

As such, those who manage DVS employees also need clear understanding of the corporate vision (i.e., what it really looks like in the marketplace), the freedom to create a departmental vision in line with the corporate mission, permission to find ways to lead others effectively, and the ability to promote the work of others over their own. We've found that many DVS executives are misunderstood because of their drive and unselfish focus and are considered weak or undisciplined. Their lack of political focus is perceived as excessive independence. Management with a VIEW will ensure that those who manage DVS employees receive the same clarity of vision, empowerment, motivation, and freedom to achieve that is required of any successful DVS employee—except now, it has the power to impact much more of the organization with growth and a focus on achieving what really matters.

In Patrick Lencioni's insightful fable *The Five Temptations of a CEO*, he outlines the five key areas of failure in management.[1] Each of his five temptations is a trade-off: as CEOs get more settled, they tend to gravitate toward what is comfortable and avoid what is crucial for the greatest productivity. They gravitate to the status quo and avoid what is difficult. Unfortunately, what is avoided is what is most necessary for growth and success. Using the focus of management with a VIEW will enable you to effectively manage the DVS employee to achieve success, for that individual as well as for the organization. These things are obviously connected; an organization will incorporate those same five critical elements for success that Lencioni identifies.[2]

Managers who treat DVS employees—and all their employees—with the elements of a VIEW will also incorporate effective initiatives that motivate employees to produce more *and* challenge the cultural obstacles that affect the health of organization and its ability to reach those higher productivity levels. Management with a VIEW requires honest observation, perseverance, integrity, standards, insight, nerve, and character. It also continually challenges management to define and stretch their vision—a vision that not only leads the DVS faction but also can lift an entire organization to new heights.

What if all this doesn't work, and there is still a feeling that the DVS employee isn't working out? Well, you might still lose an important employee, but there is a deeper threat to the organization than just an employee who doesn't fit in. When a DVS employee is terminated, it is often blamed on the political insensitivity or personal agenda that disposable visionaries can display. Often, however, it is the inability of management to step up to their own responsibilities that may be the true underlying factor. Sometimes the vision of the DVS employee is perceived as being in conflict with the vision, or lack thereof, of his or her manager. But very often the disposable visionary's vision and passion exceeds the vision, standards, and accountability that a manager is willing to provide. Conflict and challenge ensues. And when challenged and unbending, many managers cannot handle the threat. This is why it is so important for senior executives to be aware of Disposable Visionary Syndrome and to hold their managers accountable for leveraging the potential.

This points out an additional value of a DVS employee. Not only does he provide immediate and personal contributions, but also the failure to nurture and leverage his talent can point out serious issues within the organization. If a manager can bring out the best in a DVS employee, you have a hero in management and a superstar in your organization. If he can't bring out the best in a DVS employee, he is probably also failing to bring out the best in others.

So what does this mean?

The opportunity for management is to channel as well as unleash the potential of DVS employees. You can expect great achievements, but they come through dual accountability. The DVS employee will deliver, as long as management commits to providing direction, freedom, and encouragement and then stands up to defend the visionary's effectiveness.

HARVEY LOGAN

A HOLLYWOOD INSIGHT ON MANAGING DVS EMPLOYEES

In the 1970 hit movie *Butch Cassidy and the Sundance Kid*, the main characters were portrayed as free spirits and mavericks. The key DVS employee, however, was someone else: Harvey Logan (played by Ted Cassidy), a member of Butch's gang.

To refresh your memory, Butch returns to his gang to find them preparing for a train robbery. Butch's position had been usurped by Logan. To Butch's surprise, the gang is preparing to rob the *Pacific Flyer* train, an act inspired and planned by Logan.

The scene goes something like this: After learning about the plans for the train robbery, Butch responds, "You fellows got everything I told you all wrong . . . banks are safer, you know where the money is." When he tries to reestablish his personal agenda for bank robberies, he is challenged by Logan, who informs Butch that the gang has chosen to follow him now and the train robbery makes more sense to them.

(Continued)

Butch is reminded by one of the gang, "You always said one of us could challenge you, Butch," to which he replies, "Well that's 'cause I figured no one would do it."

Butch regains control only after he has surprised Logan with a strategically placed kick while they are discussing the rules of a knife fight. Interestingly, after Logan has been dispatched, Butch recognizes the potential in Logan's idea. But without the passionate planning of Logan to execute it, they fail miserably, and Butch and Sundance desert the gang and protect themselves.

Butch exemplified a manager whose vision and passion for the organization are exceeded by a subordinate: He failed to instill an understanding and passion for his own vision, and he led with words that did not always reflect what he really thought. Without direction, certain employees, especially those with DVS, will step up to identify and create a means to move the organization forward. Often a manager resents the challenge and takes whatever steps are necessary to resist ongoing confrontation and reestablish his position: namely, getting rid of the upstart subordinate. He may eventually see the insights in the employee's vision, but he lacks the perspective to carry it out. As it fails, he protects his own position.

Management with a VIEW is just the opposite of Butch's approach. An insightful manager would have provided a clear vision. Perhaps Logan would have developed a better bank robbery plan. Better yet, Butch should have appointed Logan as executive vice president of train asset procurement. But he didn't, and in the end, the most passionate and effective member of the gang was gone, and the gang fell apart.

The Hollywood story has obvious embellishments. The real Logan was five-foot-six, while Cassidy was over six-foot-five, but there is a documented story that the real Logan, also called "Kid Curry," in typical DVS fashion, later sacrificed himself for his own gang. As a posse closed in, he stayed behind to give the gang time to escape and then, already mortally wounded from a shootout, killed himself outside of Parachute, Colorado.

Chapter 11

Final Thoughts

Improvement takes time and it comes from people like you

The saving of our world from pending doom will come not from the action of a conforming majority but from the creative maladjustment of a dedicated minority.

Dr. Martin Luther King, Jr.

You were born an original. Don't die a copy.

John Mason

If you believe you have DVS, we hope that this book has been a source of encouragement. The prophet is least recognized in his own country, and the disposable visionary is often misunderstood in his own company. Rather than integration of his vision, there is conflict. And if conflict can't be accepted, then usually one party is seen as dispensable.

There are reasons for conflict; when a DVS employee is involved, they are usually good reasons. There is value in conflict. DVS employees recognize that. New ideas and paradigm shifts usually cause a lot of conflict. For some organizations or managers, the status quo itself is a goal. But not for the DVS employee. It reflects "good enough" or the path of least resistance, through which few great contributions are discovered.

Perhaps that is why they are called "breakthrough" ideas—because too often they have to break through an oppressive culture, the prevailing politics, or traditional thinking that creates more obstacles than empowerment.

The boat needs to be rocked. Like a vaccine, the body needs to be invaded so it can respond and become stronger. The DVS employee will meet resistance, but his or her passion for change, for improvement, and for the pursuit of what could be is the spark that organizations seek but often terminate. And then they ask, "Why is this boat still in the same place? Why is it moving at the same pace?"

To survive, the DVS employee must recognize the odds against which he is fighting. Staying within his or her standards, each must find ways to leverage the organizational culture, identify the champions of his or her cause, align and strategically challenge the corporate vision, and assimilate others—especially his or her supervisor and the areas of control—into a vision that is real, attainable, and verified to be worth the quest.

Look at yourself the same way you look at your customers, the market, and the world, with the same question: "How can we move to a higher level?" Be open and challenged by how you can motivate others yet also by how you might adjust to meet the internal obstacles as an influencer, not an opponent.

This also raises a final element of Disposable Visionary Syndrome: In its advanced stages, it can progress to Chronic Malcontent Syndrome. In its good form, it reflects an ongoing passion for continuous improvement, a constant challenge for enhancement of the corporate culture and how the company works. It is an ongoing sense of dissatisfaction with an organization's process, products, service, and practices, and it can be motivational, because it never settles for "good enough."

However, if the DVS employee becomes consumed with internal frustrations of the organization and begins to simply criticize and complain rather than seek out constructive alternatives, then Chronic Malcontent Syndrome can lead to the label "unproductive malcontent," which few will (and in reality, should) survive. Thus, it is up to the disposable visionary to decide for himself or herself how to focus the normal frustration: either toward constructive innovation to change the organization and its impact, or toward a self-destructive cynicism that only feeds its own frustration. Passion leads to action and attitudes, and the disposable visionary's positive or negative impact will depend on her ability to recognize and control whether she is becoming a catalyst or a cynic.

As a disposable visionary, you have a burden to bear. You bring the insights, ingenuity, perseverance, and dogged pursuit of what matters that every organization needs and wants. Unfortunately, they don't always recognize how to grow it and what it takes to leverage it. While you recognize that the organization might too often follow after the emperor's new vision statement, you also have to decide if you can step up and accept the challenge, as well as the personal sensitivity and patience necessary if you want to succeed.

From the examples outlined, it is clear that the DVS employee's passion will find its home someplace. The pursuit of dreams cannot be contained by organizations, managers, boards, or peers. It is a unique flame to create a greater success in others: in an organization and for the customer.

Here's to the DVS employee and his or her drive. And to the organizations with the insight to leverage and nurture a culture and the employees that can provide the dreams from which breakthroughs happen. Just remember, if you're going to keep rocking the boat, don't expect to always stay dry.

And so the commander, having tossed his new employee overboard, continues on his journey. Ironically, his boat continues to be rocked. But this time it is by rough waters, unpredictable winds, and unknown currents. He pulls in his sails, and he and his crew decide to wait it out.

And as they sit, he notices the enemy ships cruising along at breakneck speed. The employee he had tossed overboard had been picked up by one of their vessels. Rather than fight the weather, he sought to take advantage of the high winds. He had suggested that they tie the boats in pairs, creating stable catamarans capable of sailing through the uncertain seas, leaving the enemy behind.

The commander recognized him and wondered why he didn't make that kind of contribution while in his employ. And some people still wonder why Rome fell.

So what does this mean?

It's easy to get frustrated, especially when those calling the shots just don't get it. You know that someone needs to step up and assume ownership of change, but change is seldom realized when proposed with the attitude or arrogance of a renegade. Remaining above reproach requires self-control. Avoid bad-mouthing management or your peers. Keep your focus on what could be, and find ways to improve—rather than malign—the current situation.

Epilogue: Additional Inspiration
Encouragement for you and those around you

I quote others only in order the better to express myself.

Michel de Montaigne

The strengths of the DVS employee bring unique opportunities and challenges to any organization. In return, most organizations also bring opportunities as well as challenges to the DVS employee. As we've seen, the DVS employee is driven to contribute but faces barriers that can be obvious or subtle. But obstacles can be overcome, as we've explored through the profiles of past and present visionaries.

In closing, the following insights from the famous and not so famous are provided as encouragement to the DVS employee and the organization. They exhort visionaries to stay true to the passion of what matters and to be open to the changes that will create a more powerful partnership between you, the DVS employee, and the people you work alongside.

COMMIT TO YOUR PASSIONS

Be proud of your God-given focus to create an impact for the customer, your organization, and fellow employees.

Business leaders recognize the need for passionate visionaries who continually look for new ways to make a difference, who never settle, and who strive for the next level of "what could be." One is Alfred P. Sloan, who worked for and rose to CEO and Chairman of General Motors during its formative period from 1923 to 1956. The Sloan Foundation leads with this quote: "There has to be this pioneer, the individual who has the courage, the ambition to overcome the obstacles that always develop when one tries to do something worthwhile, especially when it is new and different."[1] Another is Walt Disney, who inspired others with the philosophy of his four C's: "Somehow I can't believe that there are any heights that can't be scaled by a man who knows the secret of making his dreams come true. This special secret, it seems to me, can be summarized in four C's. They are Curiosity, Confidence, Courage and Constancy, and the greatest of these is Confidence. When you believe in a thing, believe in it all the way, implicitly and unquestionably."[2]

Throughout the ages, many have found that passion to pursue dreams is an unbeatable trait:

Sometimes I've believed as many as six impossible things before breakfast.

Lewis Carroll

Vision is the art of seeing things invisible.

Jonathan Swift

We may affirm absolutely that nothing great in the world has been accomplished without passion.

G.W.F. Hegel

I have an almost complete disregard of precedent and a faith in the possibility of something better.

Clara Barton

If one advances confidently in the direction of his dreams, and endeavors to live the life which he imagined, he will meet with a success unexpected in common hours.

Henry David Thoreau

He did it with all his heart and prospered.

The New Testament, 2 Chronicles 31:21 KJV

COMMIT TO YOUR VALUES

Hold on to the simple, but rare character that embodies trust, selfless-ness, the pursuit of truth and what is right, and the courage to maintain standards in the light of uncertainty.

Your values make you who you are. History documents many influential people who chose to live lives of significance over worldly success. Albert Einstein, for all his impact as a physicist and theorist, provided these words on character: "Try not to become a man of success but rather to become a man of value."[3]

Other voices from the past have underscored this point:

A little integrity is better than any career.

Ralph Waldo Emerson

Hold yourself responsible for a higher standard than anybody else expects of you.

Henry Ward Beecher

A cynic is a man who knows the price of everything, and the value of nothing.

Oscar Wilde

One man with courage is a majority.

Andrew Jackson

It is a grand mistake to think of being great without goodness, and I pronounce it as certain that there was never yet a truly great man that was not at the same time truly virtuous.

Benjamin Franklin

PERSIST WHEN RESISTANCE GROWS

As you know, some organizations, managers, or peers may not be receptive to the boat-rockers, especially those with a nonpolitical stance. The environment will be tough on visionaries who want to make a difference, but new opportunities for growth will come if you reframe obstacles as challenges rather than threats. Be confident that, through the right strategies, you can work within the system to influence, change, and improve the organization.

It is perseverance that pays off. Facing obstacles with a commitment for the end vision is what separates a visionary from a dreamer. As Thomas

Edison pointed out, "Many of life's failures are people who did not realize how close they were to success when they gave up."[4] And perhaps more significantly, it is the excitement of the challenge that makes it even more rewarding since nothing of value comes easily. Ray Kroc, the man who envisioned how the McDonald's franchise would revolutionize the restaurant industry observed, "It is no achievement to walk a tightrope laid flat on the floor. Where there is no risk, there can be no pride in achievement—and, consequently, no happiness."[5]

Many others have echoed the same sentiment:

Any coward can fight a battle when he's sure of winning.

Mary Ann Evans (under the pen name George Eliot)

To escape criticism—do nothing, say nothing, be nothing.

Elbert Hubbard

A smooth sea never made a skilled mariner.

English proverb

God will not look you over for medals, degrees or diplomas, but for scars.

Elbert Hubbard

I have learned that success is to be measured not so much by the position that one has reached in life as by the obstacles which he has overcome while trying to succeed.

Booker T. Washington

This man Wellington is so stupid he does not know when he is beaten and goes on fighting.

Napoleon Bonaparte

KNOW THAT YOU ARE SPECIAL

You know what drives you, what excites you, and what has made you special. While you need to be committed to the organization and others, also continue to commit to yourself.

Two very different individuals illustrate this concept of self-knowledge; writer Jorge Luis Borges, considered by many to be the founder of postmodernist literature, and Apple cofounder, Steve Jobs. The former wrote, "Any life, no matter how long and complex it may be, is made up of a single moment—the moment in which a man finds out, once and for all, who he is."[6] Jobs offered in his 2005 commencement speech at Stanford University, "Your time is limited, so don't waste it living someone else's life. . . . Don't let the noise of other's opinions drown out your own inner voice. And most important, have the courage to follow your heart and intuition. They somehow already know what you truly want to become. Everything else is secondary."[7]

The following words remind us to hold fast to who we are and to stand up for our opinions:

> *The hottest places in hell are reserved for those who, in a time of great moral crisis, maintain their neutrality.*
>
> John F. Kennedy

> *No one can make you feel inferior without your consent.*
>
> Eleanor Roosevelt

> *It is the chiefest point of happiness that a man is willing to be what he is.*
>
> Desiderius Erasmus

> *If God had wanted me otherwise, He would have created me otherwise.*
>
> Johann von Goethe

> *Conscience is the root of all true courage; if a man would be brave let him obey his conscience.*
>
> James Freeman Clarke

RECOGNIZE THAT EXPERTS ARE OFTEN WRONG

Don't let naysayers or politically savvy experts deter you from your mission, vision, and dreams. History is filled with predictions that have failed to see what the future really holds or what the public is ready to grasp. Consider film producer Darryl Zanuck's purported 1946 dismissal, "Television won't last because people will soon get tired of staring at a plywood box every night."[8] And *Business Week*'s fateful 1968 prediction, "With over fifteen types of foreign cars already on sale here, the Japanese auto industry isn't likely to carve out a big share of the market for itself."[9] The volumes of misperceived opportunities or threats abound. Don't be dissuaded by those who are narrow of vision.

History is littered with the failed predictions of those who derided changes that they could not, or would not, understand:

Heavier than air flying machines are impossible.

Lord Kelvin, President of the British Royal Society, 1895

The horse is here to stay but the automobile is only a novelty, a fad.

The president of the Michigan Savings Bank advising Henry Ford's lawyer not to invest in the Ford Motor Co., 1903.

Who the hell wants to hear actors talk?

H. M. Warner, cofounder of Warner Brothers, 1927.

X-rays will prove to be a hoax.

Lord Kelvin, President of the Royal Society, 1883.

There is no likelihood man can ever tap the power of the atom.

Robert Miliham, Nobel Prize in Physics, 1923

KNOW WHEN TO BE FLEXIBLE

While preserving your passion and convictions, also be sensitive to the organization and the changes *you* may need to make to contribute to what really matters. Know when to push, but also when to stop. Be willing to listen carefully, learn the political subtleties and accept their reality. Appreciate the opportunities presented to use the foundation of the organization as the basis for making a difference. Maintain an optimistic attitude and look for openings. Remember, you can still alter your approach without compromising your values and vision.

It is the learner that makes the greatest impression and knowing what you don't know, for example, politics, is perhaps the most important realization. John Wooden was the basketball coach at UCLA, winning 10 national championships in a 12-year period. He observed, "It's what you learn after you know it all that counts."[10] In the heat of the moment when you are so confident in your vision for the company, also be open to a personal vision of your own growth and how to have the greatest impact. In the word of Leo Tolstoy, "Everyone thinks of changing the world, but no one thinks of changing himself."[11]

Try to consider the following when dealing within a political environment:

Whatever your advice, make it brief.

Horace

Intuition is given only to him who has undergone long preparation to receive it.

Louis Pasteur

Seeing much, suffering much, and studying much, are the three pillars of learning.

Benjamin Disraeli

He who answers before listening—that is his folly and his shame.

The Hebrew Bible, Proverbs 18:13

KEEP A CHILDLIKE OUTLOOK

Despite the obstacles, the politics, and the self-promotion so common in organizations, keep a positive and trusting outlook. Trust in others and lift them up. Believe in your dreams and in the values of doing what is right. Time and history, as well as virtue are on your side. Keep the enthusiasm, trust, and dogged ambition to pursue your dreams as children do. The world belongs to those with such a perspective.

This was noted in the late nineteenth century by physician, professor, author, and poet Oliver Wendell Holmes Sr., who offered, "Pretty much all the honest truth-telling there is in the world is done by [children],"[12] and was also observed by Alexander Graham Bell, one of the greatest inventors ever, when he said, "Never overlook the question of a child because a child looks at the world with an uncluttered mind."[13] The inward searching of a child for truth and ideas, matched with the unselfish openness to support others results in the ultimate success.

Consider these thoughts from past visionaries who understood this concept:

All my life through, the new sights of nature made me rejoice like a child.

Madame Marie Curie

For God's sake, give me the young man who has brains enough to make a fool of himself.

Robert Louis Stevenson

To endure is the first thing that a child ought to learn, and that which he will have the most need to know

Jean-Jacques Rousseau

It is the mark of a great man that he puts to flight all ordinary calculations. He is at once sublime and touching, childlike and of the race of giants.

Honore de Balzac

If you want to lift yourself up, lift up someone else.

Booker T. Washington

I was a success because you believed in me.

Ulysses S. Grant

ENCOURAGE, LEAD, AND STRIVE FOR CHANGE

As managers, don't be afraid to support conflict, challenge the status quo, or offend the environment, tradition, or powers that be. Give others the freedom to pursue, even fail in, their endeavors for what can be right. Support and encourage, rather than ridicule the nontraditional and the risky. Don't over-think. True leadership performance is often just focusing on the big picture and doing what is right. Avoid defending and pursuing the little things when visions are suppressed. Be the example of visionary and empowering leadership. Hold everyone to a level of accountability that brings each to his or her highest level. Will it offend? Perhaps, but change, and especially impactful change, is bound to offend someone. So should underperformance and political paralysis. As Eleanor Roosevelt so aptly put it, "Do what you feel in your heart to be right, or you'll be criticized anyway. You'll be damned if you do and damned if you don't."[14]

Recognize your duty as leader to dwell in the arena of discomfort and to hold your management to the standard of excellence symbolized by John F. Kennedy's summary statement on success, "Our success or failure, in whatever office we may hold, will be measured by the answers to four questions: Were we truly men of courage? Were we truly men of judgment? Were we truly men of integrity? Were we truly men of dedication? "[15]

And so, in closing, we would like to offer the following thought, which in essence summarizes the theme of this book. Offending others may not be as dangerous as holding to the status quo, or as the character of John Adams so appropriately shouted in the musical *1776*, "This is a revolution, dammit. We're going to have to offend SOMEbody!"[16]

Notes

INTRODUCTION

1. Robin Williams memorial broadcast. *Fresh Air* on National Public Radio, hosted by Dave Davies. August 12, 2014.

2. Crabtree, Steve. Gallup. "Worldwide, 13% of Employees Are Engaged at Work." October 13, 2013. http://www.gallup.com/poll/165269/worldwide-employees-engaged-work.aspx. Accessed January 1, 2015.

3. Reichheld, Frederick F., and Rob Markey. *The Ultimate Question 2.0: How Net Promoter Companies Thrive in a Customer-Driven* World (revised and expanded edition). Boston, MA: Harvard Business Press, 2011. Pp. 4–5, 52–53.

4. Goffey, Rob, and Gareth Jones. "Creating the Best Workplace on Earth." *Harvard Business Review*, May 1, 2013.

5. Charles Seaford interview, "The Future Work Project," The Economist Insights, January 1, 2015, http://www.economistinsights.com/sites/default/files/EIU-Ricoh%20Future%20Work%20Q&A%202%20-%20Charles%20Seaford.pdf. Accessed March 2, 2015. "Job insecurity is a major problem in the developed world. Ask people in Europe, for example, whether they feel secure in their work, and 13% of them will say they are 'likely' or 'very likely' to lose their job within a year. That particular number is from the EU's Third European Quality of Life Survey 2012, but it's a trend we see confirmed in our own recent research. Our latest qualitative studies suggest that job security is a top priority among the workforce. They also underline the fact that security of income is crucial for an individual's sense of positive well-being. Conversely, the effects of a lack of security are profoundly negative."

6. Goleman, Daniel. *Emotional Intelligence*. New York: Bantam Books, 1995.

7. Blickle, Gerhard, James A. Meurs, Andreas Wihler, Christian Ewen, Andrea Plies, and Susann Ginther. "The Interactive Effects of Conscientiousness, Openness to Experience, and Political Skill on Job Performance in Complex Jobs: The

Importance of Context." *The Journal of Organizational Behavior* 34 (2012): 1145–164. wileyonlinelibrary.com (accessed February 23, 2015).

8. Schmidt, Karl, Brent Adamson, and Bird Anna. "Making the Consensus Sale." *Harvard Business Review*. March 1, 2015. https://hbr.org/2015/03/making-the-consensus-sale. Accessed March 15, 2015.

9. Powell, Curtis E., and William A. Jerome, author research of 55 individuals hired in change agent roles. Results and statistics were derived from surveys conducted over a six-month investigation in 2012–13 among change agents, innovation managers, and corporate risk-takers who had left positions voluntarily or involuntarily.

CHAPTER 1

1. Warner, Burke. "TC Media Center from the Office of External Affairs." The Change Agents. May 11, 2011. http://www.tc.columbia.edu/news.htm?articleId=7889. Accessed January 31, 2015.

2. "Measuring the Effectiveness of Onboarding." Hire Gray Matter. December 15, 2014. http://www.hiregraymatter.com/measuring-effectiveness-onboarding. Accessed January 31, 2015.

3. Powell, Curtis E., and William A. Jerome. Author research 2012–13.

CHAPTER 2

1. *J. C. Penney: Main Street Millionaire*. Biography A&E Network video, 2000.

2. Sowell, Thomas. "The End of Montgomery Ward." *Capitalism Magazine*, December 30, 2000.

CHAPTER 3

1. Goleman, Daniel. *Emotional Intelligence*. New York: Bantam Books, 1995.

2. Authors Note: *In a slightly different take on the same phenomenon, research conducted in 2013 by Ryan Perry and Chris G. Sibley at the University of Auckland concluded that those who are more open to new experiences approach societal threats more rationally whereas those who are less open to new experiences react out of fear.* Perry, Ryan, and Chris G. Sibley. "Seize and Freeze: Openness to Experience Shapes Judgments of Societal Threat." *Journal of Research in Personality* 47: 677–686. Elsevier, July 2, 2013.

3. Blickle, Gerhard, James A. Meurs, Andreas Wihler, Christian Ewen, Andrea Plies, and Susann Ginther. "The Interactive Effects of Conscientiousness, Openness to Experience, and Political Skill on Job Performance in Complex Jobs: The Importance of Context." *The Journal of Organizational Behavior* 34: 1145–164. wileyonlinelibrary.com (accessed February 23, 2015).

4. Leadership IQ references: http://www.leadershipiq.com/materials/LeadershipIQ-AreSmartGoalsDumb.pdf.

5. Schmidt, Karl, Brent Adamson, and Bird Anna. "Making the Consensus Sale." *Harvard Business Review.* March 1, 2015. https://hbr.org/2015/03/making -the-consensus-sale. Accessed March 15, 2015.

6. Authors Note: *In the Blickle et al. research, this effect is even more extreme for professionals with high learning ability and low political skills than it is for PARs. It seems that for the former, being bright and conscientiousness is negatively rewarded.*

7. Leadership IQ references: http://www.leadershipiq.com/materials/LeadershipIQ -AreSmartGoalsDumb.pdf.

8. Axelrod, Alan, and Charles Phillips. *The Macmillan Dictionary of Military Biography.* New York, NY: Macmillan, 1998.

CHAPTER 4

1. Gabor, Andrea. *The Man Who Discovered Quality: How W. Edwards Deming Brought the Quality Revolution to America: The Stories of Ford, Xerox, and GM.* New York: Times Books, 1990.

2. Bianculli, David. *Dangerously Funny: The Uncensored Story of The Smothers Brothers Comedy Hour.* New York: Simon & Schuster, 2009.

CHAPTER 5

1. Gajilan, Arlyn Tobias. "The Amazing JetBlue." Fortune.com. May 17, 2003. Accessed April 2, 2010.

2. *JetBlue 2002 Annual Report.*

3. *Southwest Airlines 2002 Annual Report.*

4. *The Titan Principle E-Report 18.* June 2001, volume 2, issue 5, Titan Profile, David Neeleman, CEO JetBlue Airlines.

5. "JetBlue CEO Is Patterson Lecturer," *Northwestern University Observer Online,* April 3, 2003.

6. "A história da Azul" (in Portuguese). Azul Linhas Aereas Brasileiras. Archived from the original on May 12, 2009.

7. "Azul Brazilian Airlines Makes Successful Demonstration Flight with Amyris Renewable Jet Fuel Produced from Sugarcane." Market Watch, *Wall Street Journal.* June 19, 2012. http://www.marketwatch.com/story/photo-release-azul -brazilian-airlines-makes-successful-demonstration-flight-with-amyris-renewable -jet-fuel-produced-from-sugarcane.

8. "Azul Brazilian Airlines Makes Successful Demonstration Flight."

CHAPTER 6

1. Jonathan Edwards descendants: PrayerNet Newsletter (053097) and The Kansan Online, http://www.thekansan.com/stories/073198/rel_0731980016.html. Author: Pastor Don Myer, Newton Bible Church.

2. Liardon, Roberts. *God's Generals: The Revivalists*. New Kensington, PA: Whitaker House, 2008.

CHAPTER 7

1. Collins, James C. *Good to Great: Why Some Companies Make the Leap—and Others Don't*. New York, NY: Harper Business, 2001.

2. "Ariel Investments, UBR Radio Show Fetes 'Game Changers.'" *Black Enterprise*. August 8, 2010. http://www.blackenterprise.com/news/ariel-investments-ubr -radio-show-fetes-game-changers. Accessed July 17, 2012.

3. Lencioni, Patrick. *The Five Temptations of a CEO*. San Francisco: Jossey Bass, 1998. Lencioni outlines that the most effective management comes from a clear drive for results, the need for accountability by management, providing clarity, accepting productive conflict, and creating a sense of personal trust that comes from vulnerability and a consistency in doing what is right.

4. "Close Encounters of the Third Kind: Box Office Information." Box Office Mojo. http://www.boxofficemojo.com/search/?q=close%20encounters%20of%20 the%20third%20kind. Accessed May 26, 2014.

5. "Creating the Plymouth, Dodge, and Chrysler Minivan: The Caravan/ Voyager Development Story." www.alpar.com/model/m/history.html. Accessed February 1, 2008.

6. Conli, Roy. "Producer of Tangled." http://www.denofgeek.us/movies/16977 /roy-conli-interview-tangled-john-lasseter-treasure-planet-and-changing-disney. Accessed March 23, 2014.

7. "David Geffen." Biography.com. Accessed March 1, 2014.

CHAPTER 8

1. Rooney, David. *Military Mavericks: Extraordinary Men of Battle*. London: Cassell, 1999.

2. Lanning, Michael Lee. *The Military 100: A Ranking of the Most Influential Military Leaders of All Time*. Secaucus, NJ: Carol Pub. Group, 1996.

3. Axelrod, Alan, and Charles Phillips. *The MacMillan Dictionary of Military Biography*. New York: MacMillan, 1998.

CHAPTER 9

1. Grafton, Anthony. "Precepting: Myth and Reality of a Princeton Institution." *Princeton Alumni Weekly*, March 12, 2003.

CHAPTER 10

1. Lencioni, *The Five Temptations of a CEO*.

2. "Kid Curry and the Pro-Fun Troll Hoedown." curry.250x.com. Accessed March 11, 2008.

EPILOGUE

1. *Mission Statement, Alfred P. Sloan Foundation*. http://www.sloan.org /about-the-foundation/mission-statement. Accessed July 1, 2015.

2. *Walt Disney*. Biographies.net. STANDS4 LLC, 2015. http://www.biographies .net/people//en/walt_disney. Accessed July 1, 2015.

3. From the memoirs of William Miller, an editor, quoted in *Life* magazine, May 2, 1955; Expanded, p. 281. http://einstein.biz/biography.php. Accessed July 2, 2015.

4. Headstrom-Page, Deborah, and Sergio Martinez. *From Telegraph to Light Bulb with Thomas Edison*. B&H Publications, September 2007, p.22.

5. Kroc, Ray, and Robert Anderson. *Grinding It Out: The Making of McDonald's*. New York: Macmillan, 1992.

6. Borges, Jorge Luis. *The Life of Tadeo Isidoro Cruz (1829–1874) from Collected Ficciones*. Allan Lane The Penguin Press: The Penguin Group, 1954.

7. Steve Jobs's 2005 Stanford Commencement Address: *Your Time Is Limited, So Don't Waste It Living Someone Else's Life*, posted 10/5/11 on http://www .huffingtonpost.com/2011/10/05/steve-jobs-stanford-commencement-address _n_997301.html. Accessed January 3, 2013.

8. *Worst Tech Predictions*. www.techhive.com/article/155984/worst_tech _predictions.html, Dec 31, 2008. Accessed January 11, 2014.

9. *Business Week*, August 2, 1968. https://en.wikiquote.org/wiki/Incorrect _predictions. Accessed April 9, 2014.

10. A collection of "Woodenisms" from legendary coach John Wooden. June 5, 2010. http://www.sports.espn.go.com/ncb/news/story?id=5249709. Accessed January 12, 2013.

11. Tolstoy, Leo. *Letters to Friends on the Personal Christian Life*. The Free Age Press, 1900.

12. *Atlantic Monthly* 29: 231. *The Poet at the Breakfast-Table*. The actual quote is "I like children, —he said to me one day at table. —I like 'em, and I respect 'em. Pretty much all the honest truth-telling there is in the world is done by them."

13. Phillips, Bob. *Phillips' Awesome Collection of Quips & Quotes*. Eugene, OR: Harvest House Publishers, 2001.

14. Carnegie, Dale. *How to Stop Worrying and Start Living*. Bungay Suffolk, UK: Richard Clay, Ltd., 1944/1948.

15. The Congressional Record, January 10, 1961, vol. 107, Appendix, p. A169. *Speech to Massachusetts State Legislature delivered on January 9, 1961 in The State House, Boston, MA*.

16. Stone, Peter, and Sherman Edwards. *1776*. New York, NY: Viking Press, 1964.

Index

Accountability, 96, 103, 118, 129, 142
Adams, John, 19
Alignment, 62, 75–76, 78–80, 82–83, 121
Alliances, 79, 84, 101–102, 110
Amygdala, 18, 33
Amygdala hijack, xiv, 18
Architect/Creator style, 61, 63–64, 66, 67
Aspiration, 79–82
Azul Brazilian Airline, 56–57

Behaviors: brain-related, 18; corporate, 18; of DVS vs. PAR managers, 23, 25; instinctive, 19, 29; organizational, 3; personal, 104
Bell, Alexander Graham, 141
Benefits: of DVS employees 118, 123; economic, 109
Blickle, G., xiv, 22, 23, 24, 25
Boat-Rockers, 6–8, 13–15, 18, 22, 25, 26, 30, 33, 35, 56, 60, 67, 75, 103, 132, 133, 137
Body language, 91
Borges, Jorge Luis, 138
Bosses: agenda of, 110; giving them what they ask for, 94; helping and promoting, 94, 105; pets of, 95–97. *See also* Leadership; Management
Burke, Warner, 3
Burton, Tim, 85
Business brain functions: political function, 32; the Way, 29–32; the Whoa, 33–36; the Why, 32–33

Catmull, Ed, 86
Champions: of change, 73; finding, 101
Change: company's desire for, 3, 11, 14, 44; culture, 114; demand for, 112; effective, 110; fear of, 20; focused, 113–114; initiatives for, 81; innovative, 82, 83; model of reaction to, 44; necessary, 83; obstacles to, xv, 61, 65, 101; openness to, 62, 74, 112, 135; ownership of, 133; passion for, 132; past, 111; presentation of, 83–85; progressive, 3; resistance to, xv, 4, 5, 11, 76, 83, 112; responses to, 62; striving for, 142; value of, 22; visionary, 81; from within, 113. *See also* Ideas
Change agents, viii, 3, 4, 8, 29, 65, 75–77, 81
Change management, 45, 75

About the Authors

BILL JEROME, with coauthor Curtis Powell, has worked with more than 100 different corporations and associations, championing the concept of an "indispensable brand" and the research to identify its application. Jerome is a writer of business parables and is currently the Chief Storyteller/Marketing Director for Christian Academy School System in Louisville, Kentucky, the largest Christian school system in the country. He was previously marketing manager at Citicorp, general manager for various advertising agencies, and executive coach in vision casting and brand innovation. Bill has written and spoken for national conferences on topics including "Seven freedoms of innovation," "Creating a brand of indispensability," and "Why satisfaction studies are meaningless, and what you can do about it." He earned his Bachelor of Arts from Princeton University and Master of Management from Northwestern University.

CURTIS POWELL has a 30-year background in strategy development, marketing, research, and analytics for Fortune 500 companies and national associations in healthcare, financial services, higher education, and energy. He is the founder of MindRamp and of Endpoint Chicago, a consulting firm at the intersection of innovation, analytics, and engagement. Powell has served in marketing leadership positions for the College of American Pathologists, MidAmerican Energy, Quester Research, and Citibank NYS. He has received Addy, Telly, and AMA awards for marketing, as well as the Citicorp Service Excellence award and MidAmerican Energy's Teaming for Success award. Powell is also a composer, actor, and playwright. He earned his Master of Arts degree from the School of Speech at Northwestern University and currently lives in Chicago's Gold Coast.